ATHENS

ELENI MALAINOU
ARCHAEOLOGIST

PAPADIMAS
EKDOTIKI

CONTENTS

Publication editor:
Evangelia Chyti

Translation:
Alexandra Doumas

Design - Image processing:
Ledy Griva

Photographs:
Studio Kontos-Photostock, A Symeonakis

CTP - Printing - Binding:
EM-ES PRESS S.A.

Dim. Papadimas Reg't Co.
56-58 Char. Trikoupi St., Athens 106 80
Tel.: (++30) 210 3640235, 210 3645830
Fax: (++30) 210 3636001
e-mail: papa-ekd@otenet.gr

ISBN 978-960-6791-79-6

AKADIMIA PLATONOS SQ.
AG. GEORGIOS
KARDAMATI SQ.
AG. PAVLOS
Epigraphical Museum
National Archaeological Museum
MOUSSIO
Technical University, School of Fine Arts
VATHI
VATHIS SQ.
MS METAXOURGIO
KARAISKAKI SQ.
METAXOURGIO
METAXOURGIOU SQ.
RAMNES SQ.
EXARHION SQ.
EXARHIA
KANINGOS SQ.
National Theatre
AGIOU KONSTANDINOU
MS OMONIA
OMONIA
AG. KON/NOS
AG. GERASSIMOS
ETHNIKIS ANDISTASSIS SQ.
Opera House
ODIOU SQ.
THEATROU SQ.
CENTRAL MARKET
AG. ANARGIRI
ELEFTHERIAS SQ. (KOUMOUNDOUROU)
AG. GEORGIOS
AG. IOANIS
AG. ATHANASSIOS
ARMENIAN ORTH.
National Library
University
MS PANEPISTIMIO
Academy of Arts
Theatre Museum
AG. DIONISSIOS (CATH.)
IERA ODOS
AG. TRIADA
KERAMIKOS
Kerameikos Museum
"Gazi" Cultural Park D.E.F.A.
GAZI
PIREOS
ERMOU
SYNAGOGUE
AG. ASSOMATI
AG. PARASKEVI
AG. ANARGIRI
PSIRI
AG. KIRIAKI
AG. THEODORI
KLATHMONOS SQ.
Athens City Museum
El. Venizelos Memory Museum
Iliou Melathron (Schliemann Mansion) Numismatic Museum
AG. GEORGIOS
National Historical Museum
AG. ATHANASSIOS
MS THISSIO
The "Melina Merkouri" Cultural Centre
AFEAS SQ.
AVISSINIAS SQ.
AG. FILIPOS
MONASTIRAKI
MS MONASTIRAKI
KAPNIKAREA
MS SINDAGMA
SINDAGMA
Theseion (Temple of Hephaestus)
Stoa of Attalus Museum
Ancient Agora
Greek Folk Art Museum
Hadrian's Library
AERIDES
Andronicos Kyrrhestes Clock
AGORAS SQ.
Roman Forum
MITROPOLI
THISSIO
AG. MARINA
OBSERVATORY
Agii Apostoli
AG. PARASKEVI
AG. ANA
AG. SPIRIDON
KIMISSI THEOTOKOU
AG. ANDREAS
PLAKA
Kanelopoulos Museum
ANAFIOTIKA
Centre of Folk Art & Tradition
Jewish Museum
Arios Pagos
Erechtheion
AKROPOLIS (ACROPOLIS)
AG. NIKOLAOS
AG. GEORGIOS
PNIKA
Propylaea
Parthenonas
Herod Atticus Odeum
Dionysus Theatre
Lysikrates Monument
Zappeion Exhibition & Congress Hall
Hadrian's Arch
Temple of the Olympian Zeus
LOFOS NIMFON NIMFON HILL
AG. DIMITRIOS
DIONISSIOU AREOPAGITOU
Socrates Prison Cell
AG. SOFIA
Lalaounis Ilias Jewellery Museum
MS AKROPOLIS
Acropolis Study Centre
Acropolis Museum
MAKRIGIANI
Filopapou Monument
AG. SOTIRA
FILOPAPOU HILL
SWIMMING POOL
TENNIS COURT
AG. FOTINI
APOLONIOU SQ.
DORAS' STRATOU THEATRE
TSOKRI SQ.
AG. IOANIS
ANDREA SINGROU
KALIROIS
FILOPAPOU SQ.
MS SINGROU-FIX
AG. PAND/NAS
KOUKAKI
AG. NIKOLAOS

FINOPOULO' S HILL
AG. ELEFTHERIOS
ARGENDINIS SQ.
ALEXANDRAS
AMBELOKIPI
PANATHINAIKOS FOOTBALL STADIUM
AG. SAVAS
MS AMBELOKIPI
NEAPOLIS SQ.
NEAPOLI
LIKAVITOS THEATRE
LIKAVITOS (LICABETTUS HILL)
AG. GEORGIOS
LYCABETTUS FUNICULAR
KIFISSIAS
FIDIPIDOU
MESSOGION
AG. ANDREAS
"IPOKRATIO" HOSPITAL
MAVILI SQ.
AG. SPIRIDON
NAUTICAL HOSP.
ATHENS CONCERT HALL
Eleftherios Venizelos Museum
ELEFTHERIAS PARK
MS MEGARO MOUSSIKIS
VASSILISSIS SOFIAS
MIHALAKOPOULOU
KITSIKI SQ.
DANDE SQ.
Genadios Library
DEXAMENI
DEXAMENI SQ.
MARASLIO
EVAGELISTRIA
EVANGELISMOS
MS EVANGELISMOS
ILISSIA
ZOGRAFOU
KOLONAKI
FIL. ETERIAS SQ.
Benaki Museum
AG. NIKOLAOS
MEGALI TOU GENOUS SCHOLI SQ.
National Gallery & Alexandros Soutsos Museum
N. P. Goulandris Foundation Museum of Cycladic & Ancient Greek Art
Byzantine & Christian Museum
War Museum of Greece
P. MELA (RIGILIS) SQ.
VASSILEOS KONSTANDINOU
MADRITIS SQ.
VASSILEOS ALEXANDROU
SINGROU (SYNGROU PARK)
SINGROU
AG. ANDREAS
OULAF PALME
UNIVERSITY TOWN
AG. TAXIARHES
ATHENS CONSERVATORY
Presidential Residence
SKOUZE SQ.
Philatelic Museum
AG. SPIRIDON
Athens Stadium (Kallimarmaron)
ALSOS PANGRATIOU (PANGRATIOU PARK)
PLASTIRA SQ.
MESSOLONGIOU SQ.
PANGRATIOU SQ.
PANGRATI
IMITOU
ETHNIKIS ANDISTASSIS
AG. POLIKARPOU
AG. FANOURIOS
HRISTOU VASSILEOS CATH.
KESSARIANI
SKOPEFTIRIO
VARNAVA SQ.
PR. ILIAS SQ.
PR. ILIAS
MARTAKI SQ.
VIRONAS

ATHENS

Athens is not simply the capital of the Greek State; it is a symbol of historical and national memory, the heart of the economic, social and cultural life of the country, as well as its political centre.

This city was the bright-shining star of the ancient world, peerless in all spheres of human activity.

In one and the same period, Athens was home to many important figures, such as the tragic poets Sophocles and Euripides, the comic poet Aristophanes, the sculptor Pheidias, the historiographer Thucydides, the philosophers Socrates, Plato, Xenophon and many others.

Athens was the birthplace of the only true democracy in the world, where all decisions were made on the basis of the popular vote.

Here was created a civilization of unique quality, which even today, so many centuries later, nurtures mankind.

ATHENS, CITY OF INTELLECTUAL ACHIEVEMENT AND DEMOCRACY!

THE NATURAL ENVIRONMENT

The basin in which Athens sprawls is the largest plain in Attica, 383 square kilometres in area.

It is delimited by the mountainous massifs of Hymettos to the east, Pentele and Parnes to the north, and Aigaleo to the west, while to the south it is lapped by the sea of the Saronic Gulf.

A row of hills, among them the Tourkovounia, Lykabettos, Strephi, Ardettos and the rock of the Acropolis, divides the basin lengthwise from northeast to southwest.

To the south of the Acropolis are the hills of Philopappus, the Pnyx and the Nymphs, with a quite sizeable area of greenery which ends at the hill of Agoraios Kolonos on which stands the Hephaistion. On the northwest side of the city, in the neighbourhood of Kolonos, are the hills of Skouze and Hippios Kolonos.

The climate of Athens, principal characteristic of which is the low annual precipitation

rate, the nature of the terrain and, last, the small size of the drainage basin formed by the surrounding mountains do not favour the development of large rivers. Two small rivers flow through the basin: the Kephissos and the Ilissos.

In Attica in general, and the Athens area in particular, there are no notable mineral resources. The most fine-grained white marble in Greece was quarried on Mount Pentele. A darker marble was extracted on Hymettos, while from the area of Eleusis came a grey marble that was used mainly in architecture.

The climate of Athens is Mediterranean, main characteristics of which are warm summers with heat-waves, mild winters with many hours of sunshine, and short spring and autumn seasons. Strong north and northwest winds prevail for long periods, especially in wintertime.

Vegetation in Athens has been confined to a very few parks, in which there is a wide variety of shrubs, bushes and trees, while pine woods cover some of the city's hills. The parks and groves of Athens are home to several species of birds.

MYTH AND HISTORY

The beginnings of the history of Athens are lost in the mists of the distant past, about which nothing is certain and definite. Nonetheless, it is possible that ancient and forgotten events are crystallized in the myths and traditions. The mythology of the city of Athens is very rich and was developed and augmented in historical times, either in the service of dramatic art or for reasons of political expediency.

One myth presents the sea god Poseidon and the goddess Athena as contesting for domination of the city. Poseidon struck his trident into the rock of the Acropolis and a well of seawater appeared, whereas Athena planted the first olive tree. After a vote was taken by the Twelve Gods of Olympus, Athena was declared victor and so gave her name to Athens.

Another myth speaks of the autochthony of the Athenians, which means that they had always lived in this place. According to this, King Erichthonios was born from the Attic earth when Athena wiped with a tuft of hair the sperm of Hephaistos, who had tried to rape her, and then threw it on the ground.

Tradition has it that most of the Hellenes accepted that all four Hellenic tribes the Aeolians, the Dorians, the Ionians and the Achaians were descended from Hellen, who sired three sons Aiolos, Doros and Xouthos. Xouthos married Kreousa, daughter of King Erechtheus, and fruits of their union were Ion and Achaios. However, according to another version of the myth, the Ionian inhabitants of the land claimed that they were autochthonous and that they were named thus by their founding ancestor (genarch) Ion, who was not actually the son of Xouthos but of Apollo, from his clandestine love affair with Kreousa,

Detail from a bronze statue of Athena

Detail from a bronze statue of Poseidon

whereas Doros and Achaios were sons of Xouthos.

However, before the advent of the Ionians, Athens was inhabited by the Pelasgians. It was they who built the most ancient fortification wall, the 'Pelasgic', traces of which survive at the foot of the Acropolis rock, and they who gave the mountains and rivers of Attica their very ancient names, by which they are known to this day: Hymettos, Lykabettos, Ilissos, and so on.

Kodros, fully armed, shortly before entering battle against the Dorians

Important mythical kings of Athens were Kekrops, Pandion, Erechtheus, Aegeus and Theseus, who were commendable rulers, contributing much to the development and progress of the realm. All dwelt in the palace that stood on the Acropolis, on the site where the Erechtheion was erected later and where many of them were buried. In those times Attica was divided into twelve small cities or polities, the most notable of which were Kekropia (which subsequently became Athens), Eleusis and the four cities (*tetrapolis*) of Marathon.

Theseus is accredited with founding Athens. He relieved the city of the blood tribute it was obliged to pay to Minos, ruler of the seas and king of Crete, and was praised for his many feats or labours. Attributed to Theseus is the 'synoecism', that is, the uniting of the small cities of Attica under the one sceptre of the monarch who resided on the Acropolis. This event was commemorated hereafter by the celebration of the Panathenaia festival. After Theseus' death, the institution of kingship weakened and was soon finally abolished, when King Kodros died heroically to save Athens from invasion by the Dorians. Then, the people of the city voted that no one was worthy to succeed him and the regime of aristocracy was instituted instead of kingship.

The centuries that followed were not without political unrest. The city was disturbed mainly be rivalries between the aristocrat landowners and the wealthy merchants and craftsmen. Finally, in 594 BC, the sage Solon entered the political stage of Athens, introducing a new system of government and founding the Boule (Council) of the Four Hundred, the Ekklesia of the Demos (Citizens' Assembly) and the supreme law court, the Heliaia, as well as solving the acute problems between the poor and the rich. This constitution was kept in essence even when Peisistratos thrice seized power (560-528/7 BC). Although this astute man governed as absolute archon or tyrant, he proved himself an excellent statesman. He supported the poor, encouraged the Arts and Letters, adorned the city with many monuments, reorganized the Panathenaia festival and introduced worship of the god Dionysos.

Peisistratos was succeeded by his sons, Hippias and Hipparchos. After the assassination of Hipparchos by the tyrannicides, Harmodios and Aristogeiton, Hippias showed the true face of tyranny and was eventually overthrown in 510 BC, by the Alkmeonid family. One member of this family, Kleisthenes, neutralized his political opponents and imposed a series of administrative reforms, so opening the way for a more representative system of government. He limited the power of the aristocrats in all sectors, supplemented Solon's legislation, increased the number of deputies to the Boule (*bouleutai*) to five hundred; in short, he prepared the ground for the establishment of Pericles' Democracy.

In 490 BC, the Persian king Darius decided to punish the Athenians for supporting the revolt of the Greek cities of Asia Minor against his rule. His large army landed at Marathon, where the Athenians were waiting, led by General (*strategos*) Miltiades and aided only by 1,000 Plataiaians. In the battle that ensued, 'The Athenians fighting at Marathon, on behalf of all the Greeks, vanquished the force of the gold-clad Persians', as Simonides wrote in his famous epigram.

Ten years later, the Persians invaded Greece again, led by their new king. Xerxes. After the battle of Thermopylai, they entered the evacuated city of Athens, put the Acropolis to the torch and destroyed everything. Then, Xerxes climbed to the top of Mount Aigaleo and from his throne watched the naval battle of Salamis in the straits between Attica and the island, which ended with the destruction of his fleet by the Athenian *strategos* Themistocles. This far-sighted statesman believed that Athens' future was the sea and foresaw the conflict between Athens and Sparta. For this reason he fortified Athens and its port, the Piraeus, with impregnable walls, built the harbour and enhanced Athens as a major maritime power. His public works and fortifications were continued by his successor Kimon.

Kimon was succeeded by Pericles, who 'thundered and lightened, and touched the emotions of all Hellas' when he spoke, and was named Olympian. Elected archon by the citizens of Athens in 461 BC, under his administration, which lasted until his death in 429 BC, the city's power and, primarily, its cultural achievements in the Arts and Letters, attained their glorious zenith, while concurrently the democratic body politic was integrated and established. However, that which made Pericles immortal is the construction of the

Copy of the sculptural group of the Tyrannicides, Harmodios and Aristogeiton

magnificent monuments on the Acropolis, which even today dazzle the whole of the civilized world. That is why when we speak of 'ancient Athens' our thoughts turn automatically to the city and the Acropolis in the Golden Age of Pericles. All domains of intellectual activity flourished in the fifth century BC: philosophy with Anaxagoras and Socrates, history with Herodotus and Thucydides, and, above all, dramatic poetry, with Aeschylus, Sophocles and Euripides.

This century of victories, glories and cultural achievements was to conclude miserably with the internecine strife between Athens and Sparta, the Peloponnesian War (431-404 BC). Outcome of this was the defeat of Athens, leaving its political life in turmoil, crushing its naval and military power, and decimating the whole of Hellas. Despite the devastation, however, the cultural life of Athens continued, with such distinguished figures as the philosopher Plato, the historiographer Xenophon, the sculptor Praxiteles and the orators Demosthenes and Lykourgos. And it was this culture that was later admired by Alexander the Great, who, although he vanquished the Athenians and their allies at Chaironeia (338 BC), respected Athens and honoured her. Indeed. He sent the shields from the booty of the battle of the Granikos river and hung them on the cornice of the Parthenon.

In 146 BC the Romans subjugated Greece. In the early years of Roman rule, Athens suffered greatly, particularly when Sulla (86 BC) destroyed the city and the harbour of the Piraeus, and plundered countless artworks which he dispatched to Rome. On the contrary, during imperial times, and especially in the second century AD, thanks to the emperor Hadrian, who held the city in high esteem, as well as to citizens such as Herodes Atticus,

Athena sees Erichthonios coming out of the open basket, amidst the snakes

Athens one more enjoyed a heyday. Many new splendid buildings were erected monuments, temples, an aqueduct, the Library of Hadrian, the Olympieion and the Odeum of Herodes Atticus, to name but a few.

The city endured another major destruction in AD 267, at the hands of the Herul hordes, but even after this incursion it continued to be considered the intellectual hub of the ancient world, thanks to its illustrious past and its renowned schools of rhetoric and philosophy. In these last studied the Fathers of the Church, Basil the Great and Gregory of Nazianzus. With the closure of these schools, by edict of the emperor Justinian in AD 529, Athens' glory faded. Over the years, the city dwindled into a small provincial town and followed the fortunes of the rest of Greece.

For centuries little was known of its history because the Byzantine administration showed it no particular favour. The succession of conquerors Franks, Catalans, Venetians, Florentines and Ottoman Turks who came after were oblivious to its splendid past and had no idea of the sanctity of the rock of the Acropolis, where they installed their palaces and harems, their bureaucracies and their arsenals. Thus, as time passed, wars, fanaticism and ignorance left their indelible and terrible marks on the masterpieces of ancient Hellenic civilization.

In 1821 the Greek War of Independence broke out, and in 1834, when Athens was declared capital of the Greek State, there were no more than two hundred habitable houses in the town, while the Acropolis was a heap of ruins.

Works on clearing and restoring the monuments commenced right away. Athens grew gradually at first and rapidly later, and is today a megalopolis which, together with its suburbs and the port of Piraeus, is home to four and a half million people.

The Arch of Hadrian

The River Ilissos, Philopappus Hill in the background, the Acropolis, the temple of Zeus Olympios and Lykabettos Hill. (E. Dodwell, *Views in Greece*, London 1821)

THE ACROPOLIS

The word Acropolis is a compound noun, which means the highest point (Gr. *akro*) of the city (Gr. *polis*). Almost all Greek cities had their acropolis or citadel. There they had their sanctuaries and there the inhabitants felt safe in times of war.

Athens was no exception to this rule and from the prehistoric era had its own Acropolis, which to this day is the paramount reference point of ancient Hellenic civilization and symbol of the city of Athens.

The rock of the Acropolis is polygonal in shape and covers an area of approximately 30,000 square metres. Its height above the level of the surrounding space is 70 metres.

Excavations on the slopes and at the foot of the Acropolis have uncovered traces of settlement dating back to the Neolithic Age (4th millennium BC). The finds dating from the Early and the Middle Bronze Age are more numerous and indicate the presence of buildings on top of the Acropolis and of settlements on its slopes. From the Late Bronze Age or Mycenaean period (13th-12th century BC), large parts of the Cyclopean wall that girt the sacred rock survive, as well as manmade terraces and remains of the royal palace (*megaron*).

In the Archaic period, the temple of Athena known as the '*Archaios Naos*' (= old temple) and the Archaic Parthenon or Hekatompedon (100 Attic feet in length) were built on the Acropolis.

During the tyranny of Peisistratos, a monumental entrance (*propylaia*) was constructed on the Acropolis, which had in the meanwhile been transformed from seat of the king to a locus of worship, and the Archaios Naos of Athena, the ruins of which lie adjacent to the Erechtheion, was adorned with sculptural decoration.

In the Golden Age of Pericles, the Acropolis was a great sanctuary in which, principally, Athena was worshipped, as goddess of wisdom, crafts and peace, but also a martial deity who bestowed victory on the city named after her. Between the Erechtheion and the Propylaia stood a colossal statue (said to have been 16 metres high) of Athena Promachos (= first in battle), protectress of the city, a work of the sculptor Pheidias.

ACROPOLIS
TEL.: 2103210219
OPEN DAILY: 08.00-20.00 HRS
APPLIES TO THE ARCHAEOLOGICAL SITES: ACROPOLIS, THEATRE OF DIONYSOS, SANCTUARY OF ZEUS OLYMPIOS, ANCIENT AGORA, ROMAN AGORA, LIBRARY OF HADRIAN, KERAMEIKOS

The 'Varvakeios Athena', small-scale copy of Pheidias' statue of Athena

THE PROPYLAIA

The entrance to the Acropolis was always on its west side. Already in the Mycenaean period (1600-1100 BC) there was a pathway leading up to the entrance, which was guarded by a might tower.

In the time of Peisistratos (6th century BC) a magnificent propylon was built on the site of the entrance of prehistoric times. This building was destroyed in the Persian attack of 480 BC and very few parts of its foundations survive on the southeast side of the Propylaia of Mnesikles.

The Greeks used the term '*propylon*', in the singular, when referring to a simple antechamber at the entrance of a sanctuary or a *megaron*, and '*propylaia*', in the plural, when referring to a more monumental entrance with more than one gateway, such as those of the Acropolis, Eleusis and Epidauros.

The Propylaia of the Acropolis were built in the time of Pericles, by the distinguished architect Mnesikles, to replace the propylon of the Peisistratids. They are a large and imposing building, befitting the sanctity of the rock and the beauty of the monuments that grace it. Their splendour rivals that of the Parthenon and was hymned by authors and orators, by friends and foes of Athens.

Construction of the Propylaia commenced in 437 BC and stopped in 432 BC, due to the threat of the Peloponnesian War. The monument was never finished, as can be seen from the square lifting bosses on the blocks of marble, which were not trimmed off the outside wall.

The Propylaia are built of white Pentelic marble, enlivened at certain points with grey

Eleusinian marble, which emphasizes characteristic features. They comprise a central rectangular building (24 x 18.20 m.) and two wings, one to the north and one to the south. The central building is divided into three parts by two rows of Ionic columns a total of six, while a marble wall perpendicular to these divides it into two façades, one east and one west. On each façade there are six Doric columns and a pediment. This union of the Doric and the Ionic order is one of the elements that impart such harmony and symmetry to this architectural creation. In this wall are five gateways, the central and largest of which (7.37 x 4.18 m.) was the main entrance.

The ceiling consisted of marble beams, supported on the walls and the Ionic columns, and of marble coffering. From traces of the metal and painted stars that were affixed to the coffers, we can imagine in our mind's eye the phantasmagoric ceiling, which will have looked like a blue sky spangled with golden stars.

The north wing was occupied by a large hall, the so-called *Pinakotheke* (Gallery of Paintings), the walls of which were adorned with paintings by leading artists of the fifth century BC, such as Polygnotos. Mnesikles intended to construct an analogous hall in the south wing too, but it seems that he met with the reaction of the priests of the nearby sanctuaries of the Graces and of Athena Nike. So, he altered his plans and built here a smaller, open room.

In addition to the masterpieces of painting, the Propylaia were adorned with sculptures, such as the statue of Hermes Propylaios, the Graces (Charites fair divinities full of sweetness and grace, who were present at the festivals) and the bronze Lioness (Gr. *leiana*) by Amphikrates, a monument in honour of Leiana, mistress of Aristogeiton, who

Reconstruction of the Propylaia

The pedestal of Agrippa

Detail of the Propylaia

although tortured by the tyrant Hippias kept her silence and did not betray the tyrannicides.

In Classical times access to the Propylaia was via a smooth ramp, 80 metres long and 20 metres wide. This facilitated the ascent not only of people but also of pack animals, which were used to transport materials, and of the cattle and sheep destined for sacrifice in the large processions, such as that of the Panathenaia. Later, in the reign of Emperor Claudius (AD 41-54), a monumental staircase was built, and in the third century AD the gateway that is known today as the Beulé Gate, after the French archaeologist Ernst Beulé, who brought it to light in excavations.

Half way up the access ramp looms a high pedestal of Hymettan marble, which was built in the second century BC and initially held a four-horse chariot (*quadriga*) of a benefactor of Athens, perhaps Eumenes II, King of Pergamon (197-158 BC). In the late first century BC this was replaced by the *quadriga* of another benefactor of Athens, Marcus Vipsanius Agrippa (63-12 BC), Roman general and son-in-law of Augustus.

In the Byzantine Age the Propylaia became the seat of the Archbishopric of Athens. Later, the Franks installed in them the administrative services of the Duchy of Athens. The Florentine nobleman Nerio Acciaioli used them as his residence and built onto the south wing a tall square tower (Koulas), which was pulled down in 1875. In the Ottoman period this was where the Turkish garrison commander lived, while the Propylaia were turned into an arsenal and gunpowder store. In 1645 lightening struck the Propylaia, igniting the gunpowder and causing irreparable damage. This was the final blow to the masterpiece by Mnesikles.

THE TEMPLE OF ATHENA NIKE

The charming Ionic temple of Athena Nike stands on a tower to the southwest of the Propylaia, offering a wonderful view over the Saronic Gulf, Piraeus, Salamis, Aegina, the Peloponnese, Mount Aigaleo and Mount Poikilon. For this reason, already from prehistoric times this strategic location was used as a surveillance post for sighting possible raids, mainly from the sea. A tall tower was built on the same spot in Late Mycenaean times, in order to control the access and the gateway to the citadel.

At this point we cannot but remember the captivating tales from the time of King Aegeus, which are lost in the mist of myths and legends. Of the ship with the black sails of mourning, which departed for Crete each year, to pay the tribute Athens owed to Minos. And the tribute

The temple of Athena Nike

was the flower of Athenian youth, seven boys and seven girls, who were lost to Crete, where they played fatal games with bulls. It was said that they were swallowed by the Minotaur. Of Theseus, who one year went with the human tribute, slew the monster and then, with the help of the princess Ariadne, managed to come out of the Labyrinth, the daedalic palace of Knossos. Of how, on his return voyage to Athens, perhaps from sorrow that the god Dionysos had kept his beloved Ariadne on Naxos, Theseus forgot to unfurl the white sails of victory on the ship. And so the aged Aegeus, sitting in this tower, espied the black sails out at sea, and in his grief lost his mind and leapt from the rock.

The Nike *'Sandalizousa'* (adjusting her sandal), from the parapet of the temple of Athena Nike

The Nike (Victory) who was worshipped here was identified with Athena, who was worshipped on the entire rock. And because the *xoanon*, the wooden cult effigy of Athena, which represented the goddess standing and holding a pomegranate in one hand and a helmet in the other, was without wings, she was called the 'wingless Nike'. It was then said that the Nike had flown to Athens but that because she should never leave the city, she no longer needed wings.

From as early as the Archaic period, a small temple of poros stone had been built to Athena Nike upon the Mycenaean tower. This was destroyed during the Persian invasion in 480 BC, along with other sanctuaries.

Building of the Classical temple began after 421 BC, in a lull in the Peloponnesian War, the so-called 'Peace of Nikias'. Nikias was an Athenian statesman renowned for his honesty and wisdom, who tried to put an end to the war by contracting a peace treaty with the Spartans, in 421 BC. Kallikrates, who had also participated in the construction of the Parthenon, was commissioned to draw the plans for the temple.

Built of Pentelic marble, the temple of Athena Nike is amphiprostyle and tetrastyle, that is, with four Ionic columns on the east front and four on the west. It is 8.27 m. long and 5.44 m. wide, while the height of the columns is 4.66 m. The three-stepped crepis on which it stands enhances the Attic grace and elegance that typify this edifice.

Represented on the east side of its frieze were Olympian gods. Athena held pride of place, standing between Zeus and Poseidon, while Aphrodite and Eros, and Demeter and Kore flank the group. Perhaps they are discussing the battles being fought on the other three sides of the frieze: battles between Greeks and Persian cavalry, as well as battles between Greeks and other hoplites (infantrymen), which cannot be more precisely interpreted.

Unfortunately a part of the frieze has been destroyed, while the reliefs from the north and west sides are presently in the British Museum and replicas have been placed on the temple.

In the late fifth century BC, a parapet about 1 metre high was built on three sides of the tower (north, west and south). The outer face of the parapet was decorated with reliefs of exquisite art, which are in the Acropolis Museum.

Amphora with representation of Athena in panoply

The excellent sculptors, now anonymous, were evidently elated by Athens' military successes and envisioned Nikai everywhere, serving the goddess Athena. Ethereal, airy and in perpetual motion, the winged Nikai enthusiastically speed to prepare the animals for sacrifice and the trophies for victorious battles against barbarians, in order to offer them to the goddess Athena, who waits at the centre, seated on a rock. The most charming of them appears to be loosening her sandal, so as to step barefoot on the altar. Her clinging garment, as if wet, reveals her lovely, lissome body, as is characteristic of the 'Rich Style' in sculpture, which dominated in the last quarter of the fifth century BC.

The Nike temple was demolished in 1687 by the Ottoman Turks, who used its building material in fortification works. Fortunately, these *spolia* were discovered and identified in 1835, and it was thus possible to reconstruct the monument. A second restoration was carried out in 1940, while a third has been in progress since 2004.

THE PARTHENON

The Parthenon stands on the highest and most conspicuous point of the sacred rock of the Acropolis. This temple is not the first Parthenon to have been erected here. As can be seen in its foundations, the *'Archaios Naos'* that was destroyed by the Persians in 480 BC, prior to its completion, was also built of marble but was not as long and wide as the present Parthenon, and had six columns on the fronts. However, traces also exist of an even earlier temple of poros stone. In 449 BC, Pericles commissioned plans for the final Parthenon from Iktinos, who collaborated with Kallikrates, architect of the temple of Athena Nike. Supervisor of the whole project was Pheidias, close friend and artistic adviser of Pericles, as well as the creator of the entire sculptural decoration of the monument. Construction of the Parthenon started in 447 BC and ended just nine years later, in 438 BC. On the occasion of the Panathenaia festival of that year, the Athenians beheld for the first time Pheidias' ivory-and-gold statue of Athena. The rest of the sculptural decoration was completed later, by 432 BC.

Initially, the square chamber behind the cella of the temple was named Parthenon, that is the chamber of Athena Parthenos, the Virgin goddess. From the fourth century BC onwards, the name was applied to the whole building, which was previously called the Great Temple (*Megas Naos*) or simply the Temple (*Naos*).

The Parthenon is constructed entirely of Pentelic marble. A peripteral temple in the Doric order, with an amphiprostyle cella, it is 69.51 metres long and 30.86 metres wide. There are eight columns of height 10.45 metres on each front and seventeen (double the number plus one) on each long side, that is a total of 46 columns, because the corner ones are counted twice. Each column has 20 flutes and the diameter is not the same for its whole height. A little way above the base the columns appear to swell and above this to become more slender as they approach the column capital. In other words, they appear to curve slightly under the weight they bear but to resist this strongly, as if alive. This curvature, which is called *entasis*, endows the monument with grace, elasticity and vitality.

The axis of the columns is not perpendicular to the stylobate. All incline towards the centre and the four corner ones even more, with a resultant deviation of about 7 centimetres. In this way, the impression that some large buildings give that their upper part 'escapes' outwards into the void is avoided, and the building acquires greater stability to possible earthquakes. Moreover, because the four corner columns, visually isolated in the void, would seem to be slimmer than the others, they were given a larger diameter and the distance between them and the adjacent columns was reduced. The horizontal line of the stylobate and the steps on the long side is slightly curved. The level in the middle is 11 centimetres higher than at the two ends and this curvature is transmitted throughout the temple, up to the roof. Thus the problem of rainwater is solved, which is shed outside the building and does not form pools on the stylobate and the steps of the crepis.

Supported upon the epistyle is the diazoma with the triglyphs and the metopes. The roof was of timber with marble tiles. Visible on the epistyle of the east side, above the columns, are square holes, in which were hung 22 Persian shields, booty of Alexander the Great from the battle of Granikos.

Many parts of the 92 metopes, the two pediments and the Ionic frieze of the cella have survived, most of which are in the British Museum and a few in the Acropolis Museum. Represented on the metopes of the east side were scenes of Gigantomachy, the battle between the gods and the Giants; on the south side are scenes of Centauromachy, the battle between the Lapiths and the Centaurs; on the west are scenes of Amazonomachy, the battle between Theseus and the Amazons; and on the north are scenes from the Trojan War.

Of the fifty or so statues that adorned the two pediments of the temple, several fragments survive, which are presently in the British Museum. Of the few in the Acropolis Museum,

The 'pitcher-bearers' *(hydriaphoroi)*, from the north frieze

Horsemen, from the north frieze

the most complete is the superb group of Kekrops and his daughter. The subject of the east pediment was the birth of Athena from the head of Zeus, while that of the west pediment was the quarrel between Athena and Poseidon.

However, The most original and indeed unique sculptural decoration of the temple is the Ionic frieze that surrounded the cella. Of overall length 160 metres and including about 600 figures of gods, men and animals, it is a remarkable composition representing the procession of the Panathenaia. The procession starts from the west side with the preparation of the horsemen. In parallel along the north and the south side, the procession of men and women holding offerings, and a host of animals for sacrifice makes its way to the Acropolis. Represented on the east side is the procession at its destination, with the gods of Olympus in the middle, who have come to honour the celebration.

Unlike most temples, the interior of the Parthenon was not divided into three parts but into four: the pronaos, the cella, a square chamber behind the cella, and the opisthodomos. The pronaos and the opisthodomos were prostyle, with six Doric columns each. The cella proper was called *hekatompedos*, which means that it was 100 Attic feet in length (approx. 30 metres) and was divided into three aisles by two two-tier colonnades that surrounded the chryselephantine statue of Athena Parthenos at the far end.

Detail from the northwest corner of the temple

Reconstruction of the Parthenon

This statue, yet another wonderful creation of Pheidias, was 10 metres tall. Its core was of wood to which were affixed pieces of ivory for the goddess's flesh and beaten gold sheet for her garments, helmet and weapons. Athena was represented as a martial goddess, her helmet elaborately decorated with sphinxes and winged horses. On her chest she wore the aegis (a shield of goatskin which was given to her by Zeus) and in her right hand she held a winged Nike 2 metres high. With her left hand she held a shield, on the inside of which was coiled the '*oikouros ophis*' (house snake) of the Acropolis. This same surface was adorned with a representation of Gigantomachy, while on the outer surface was a representation of Amazonomachy. Represented on the soles of the goddess's sandals was Centauromachy and on the base of the statue was the birth of Pandora, with gold figures affixed to the marble. Nothing has survived of this statue, which was lost in the Early Byzantine period.

The Parthenon was damaged by various interventions, when it was converted into a church of the Holy Wisdom of God and later of the Virgin Atheniotissa, in the Byzantine Age. The Franks turned it into a Catholic church in 1204, and the Turks turned it into a mosque in 1466 and into a gunpowder store sometime later. On 26 September 1687, the Venetian doge Francesco Morosini bombarded the Acropolis and one shell struck the Parthenon, reducing Iktinos' masterpiece to a wretched ruin. In 1802, Lord Elgin removed many of the sculptures from the Parthenon and subsequently sold them to the British Museum. Works on conserving and restoring the monument began in 1975 and still continue.

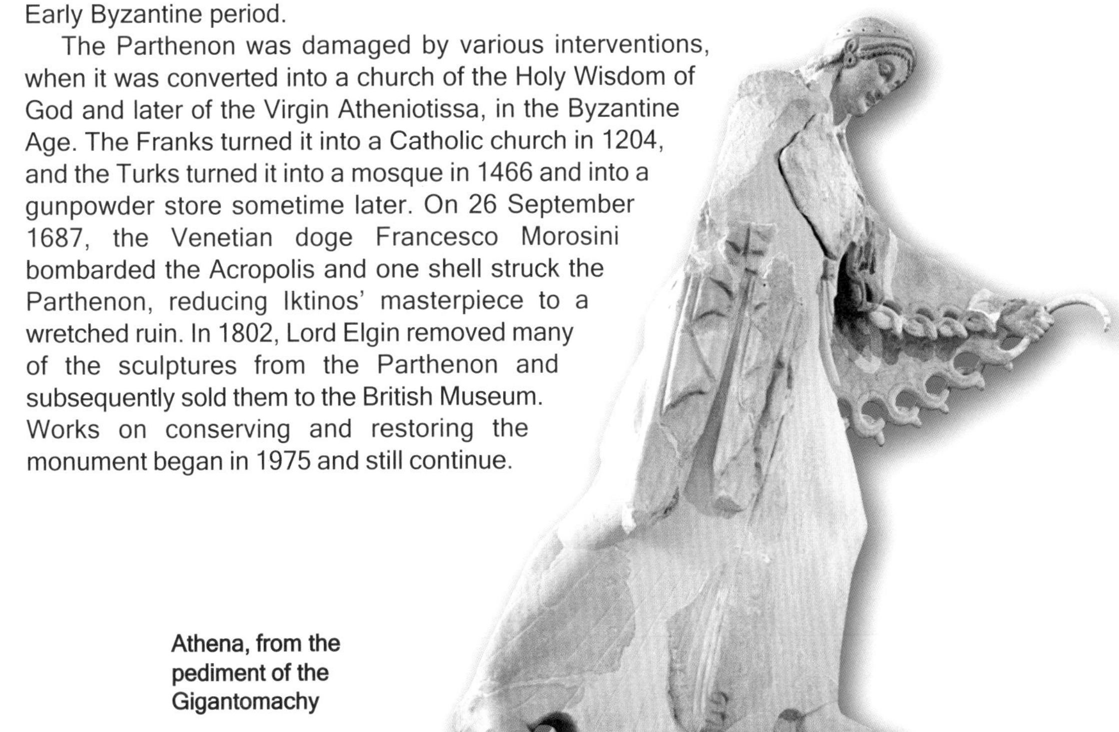
Athena, from the pediment of the Gigantomachy

THE ERECHTHEION

On the north side of the Acropolis stands the Erechtheion, which takes its name from Erechtheus, mythical king and hero of Athens. This edifice is impressive by virtue of its Attic elegance and grace. This is the most sacred space on the Acropolis, which hosted the cults of many deities, such as Gaia, Hephaistos, Athena and Poseidon, and of heroes, such as Kekrops, Erechtheus and Boutes. The large number of gods and heroes worshipped here, as well as the considerable difference in the height of the ground presented difficult problems, which the unknown architect had to resolve. For this reason the temple displays many architectural singularities, although in the end it gives the impression of one harmonious unity.

The Erechtheion was built of Pentelic marble, during the Peloponnesian War. Construction began in 421 BC and the temple was completed 15 years later, in 406 BC, by the architect Philokles.

The east porch (*prostasis*) with the six slender Ionic columns led into the temple of Athena Polias (= protectress of the city). Above the three-zone Ionic epistyle there was a frieze of dark Eleusinian marble, to which were affixed reliefs in white marble. Inside the marble cella stood the *xoanon* of the goddess, her cult effigy in olive wood, which was believed to have fallen from heaven to honour the city. This *xoanon* was robed in the ceremony of the Panathenaia with the peplos woven by young maidens of Athens. Before it was set the gold lamp with the undying flame, which was filled with olive oil only once a year, work of the sculptor Kallimachos.

On the north side of the temple there was a splendid Ionic propylon with six richly decorated columns. This led into the west part of the cella, which was dedicated to

Poseidon, Hephaistos and the hero Boutes.

The coffered ceiling of the propylon is a masterpiece of Attic art, as is the majestic portal frame carved with palmettes and rosettes, which were all painted and embellished with gilded metal ornaments. In the ceiling is a hole that was permanently open, because it was believed to have been made by Zeus' thunderbolt, which struck Erechtheus, or by Poseidon's trident when he quarrelled with Athena. Correspondingly, there are three holes in the floor, like traces of a trident. Worshippers offered libations here.

The most original and wonderful architectural creation of the Erechtheion is the porch of the Korai, situated on its south side. It is better known as the porch of the Karyatids, which name has prevailed since Roman times, perhaps because the beauty of the female figures recalls that of maidens of the city of Karyai in Laconia, who performed ritual dances in honour of Artemis.

The Karyatids are six very beautiful girls carrying on their head a kalathos decorated

Karyatid

Erechtheion, detail

with Ionic cymatium, which uphold the ceiling of the prostasis. They wear an ankle-length pleated chiton and have one leg flexed, which imparts an easy grace, as if they feel nothing of the weight of the roof they support. They appear to be identical but closer inspection reveals that each one has her own different personality. However, in all the hair hangs on the shoulders, so that the weak point of the neck of the statue is reinforced. Of the six Karyatids, the five that stood on the monument until a few years ago are exhibited in the Acropolis Museum, while the sixth, which was taken by Lord Elgin, is in the British Museum.

The Porch of the Karyatids

Reconstruction of the Erechtheion

OTHER SANCTUARIES

The visitors who passed through the Propylaia into the space of the Acropolis beheld on the south side, to his right, the sanctuaries of Athena Hygieia and of Artemis Brauronia (this epithet indicating that her cult had been introduced from the sanctuary of Brauron), as well as the Chalkotheke, not far from the Parthenon.

The Chalkotheke was an oblong building fronted by a portico with colonnade, which was built *circa* 400 BC. In it were kept precious metal *ex-votos*, bronze weapons and rams of ships, all products of the craft of which Athena Ergane was patron goddess.

Dominating the left side, opposite the Propylaia, was the colossal bronze statue of Athena Promachos by Pheidias, which together with its base was 9 metres high. It was said that the tip of the goddess's spear, which glinted in the sun, was visible from the sea.

West of the Erechtheion was the Pandroseion, that is the sacred precinct (*temenos*) of the nymph Pandrosos, daughter of Kekrops. Here, Athena Pallas offered the great gift to her city: the olive tree. The tree we see today was planted on the site of the ancient one by Queen Olga, in the early twentieth century. Next to the olive tree was the very ancient tomb of one of the mythical kings of the city, perhaps Kekrops.

On the site of the former Acropolis Museum was the sanctuary of one other mythical king of Athens, Pandion.

A short distance beyond, northeast of the Parthenon, was the temenos of Zeus Polieus.

Also visible are the foundations of a circular Ionic temple of 27 BC, dedicated to the goddess Roma and the emperor Augustus.

In and amongst all these sanctuaries stood a host of *ex-votos*, statue groups and many other works of art.

Scale model of the Acropolis in the 2nd century AD.

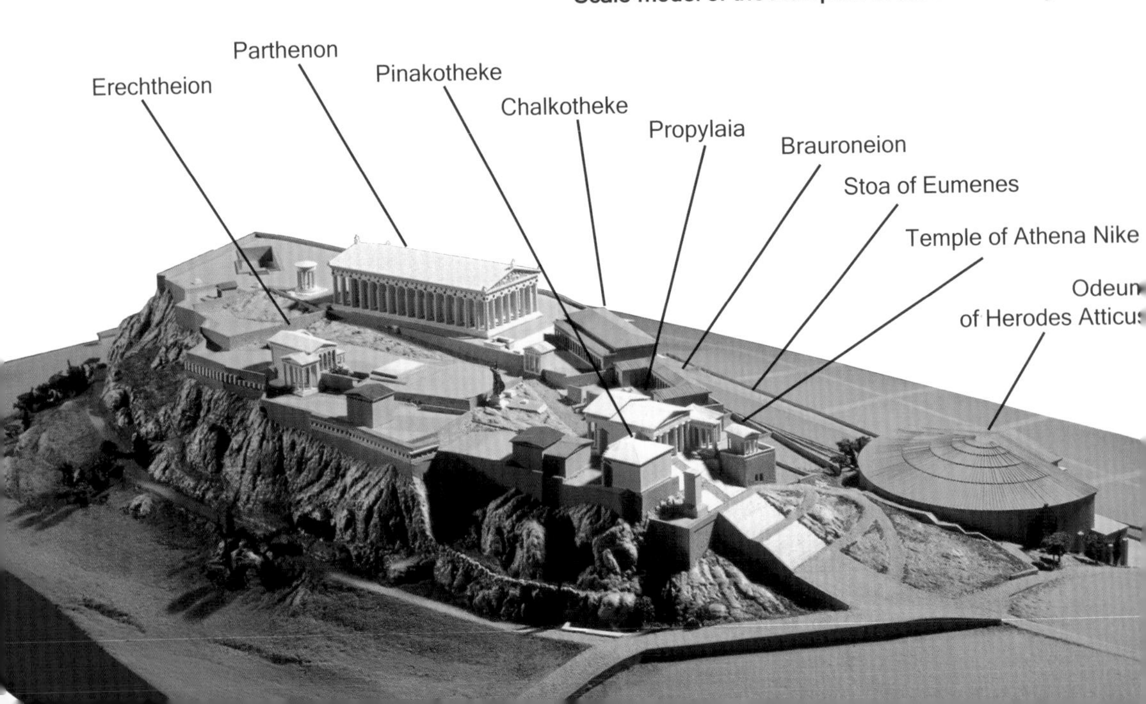

THE NEW ACROPOLIS MUSEUM

The first Acropolis Museum was founded in 1878. The new Acropolis Museum was inaugurated on 20 June 2009. It is located about 300 metres southeast of the Parthenon, in the historical Makrygiannis neighbourhood.

As visitors enter the museum, they pass across a glass floor, below which are preserved and enhanced the finds brought to light in the excavations occasioned by the earth-removal works for the foundations of the new museum. It is estimated that in about one year visitors will be able to walk around this ancient quarter of the city.

We pass through the museum foyer into the first gallery, which is the Gallery of the Slopes of the Acropolis. Spacious and with a glass-floored ramp, it alludes to the ascent to the Sacred Rock. On one side are finds from the sanctuaries at the foot of the Acropolis and on the other are objects used in daily life by the rich persons who lived there. At the centre of the gallery, two terracotta Nikai welcome the visitors.

At the far end of the room is a staircase with glass treads, at the top of which are displayed the sculptures from the pediment of the Hekatompedon or the Archaic Parthenon. At the centre of the poros frieze, painted in vivid colours, are two lions attacking a bull. At the left edge, Herakles conquers Triton, a sea monster with the head of a man and the tail of a fish. On the right side of the pediment, a coiled three-bodied daemon, with three human heads and torsos ending in a snake-tail, watches the struggle. In all likelihood this figure is Nereus, also a sea monster, who was capable of metamorphosis, which is probably hinted at by the symbols he holds in the hands of each of the three torsos: water, fire and a bird (a clever way of denoting air).

We have already entered the Gallery of the Archaic Works, in which visitors can move freely among the statues, conspicuously positioned so that details of their body or their hairstyle can be seen to advantage. At the centre is the Kritias Boy and around it are dozens of Korai and fewer Kouroi, with their haughty demeanour, and beside them are the famous Horsemen and votive plaques.

The Kritias Boy (480 BC) is a marble statue of a young athlete, with refined facial features and handsome body. His hair is wound into a circlet and the eyes were inlaid in another material. In this work the sculptor frees the body from its static form.

The Korai are votive statues which Athenians offered to their goddess for her delight - in fact, the Greek word for statue (*agalma*) derives from the verb to delight (*agallomai*) - and since this was their mission, they had to smile. The first Korai were created in the workshops of Ionia in the sixth century BC and were much liked by Athenian artists, who continued their production here. Distinguished by their beauty and richly coloured, they have elaborate hairstyles, are dressed in chiton and lavishly draped himation, and wear jewellery.

Striking and coquettishly dressed is the large Kore, while visitors cannot fail to notice the Kore with the almond-shaped eyes and the restrained serious smile. The Peplophoros Kore, as her name indicates, wears a plain Doric peplos over a fine chiton. And although the robes are straight, without pleats and folds, and at first glance the

The 'Rampin' Horseman

The Chian Kore

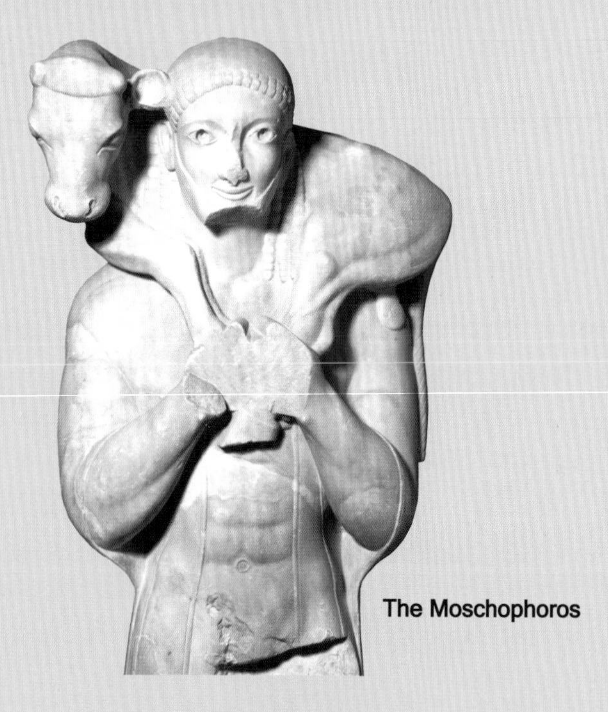
The Moschophoros

statue appears to be very archaic, the artist has succeeded, with the smooth modelling and a few curves, in suggesting the lines of her body and giving her life, which culminates in her radiant smiling face with beaming gaze, and her wavy hair on which traces of red pigment are visible.

The Chios Kore, opulent in her embroidered garment and bedecked with jewellery, still preserves much of her original coloration. The tallest Kore, 2 metres high, more serious and majestic than the others, is attributed to the sculptor Antenor. Important too is the unsmiling Kore ('La Boudeuse'), which heralds the period of the 'Severe Style' and is known as the Kore of Euthydikos, after the name of its dedicator.

The famous Moschophoros (*ca* 570 BC), sculpted in Hymettan marble, is a votive statue representing a man named Rombos, who comes from a *demos* in Attica to offer the calf for sacrifice to the goddess. The figure strongly resembles contemporary Kouroi and like them has the left leg to the fore and the distinctive Archaic smile. The eyes were inlaid in coloured stones and although these are now missing the countenance is expressive and full of vitality, in contrast to the expressionless face of the animal, which is resigned to its fate.

Exhibited in the same gallery is the best known of the Archaic Horsemen of the Acropolis, the Rampin Horseman (*ca* 550 BC). It is named after the French connoisseur to whose collection the head formerly belonged. This head is now in the Louvre, while

Nereus or Three-bodied Daemon

The ‘Mourning Athena’

a cast of it has been placed here. The body of the rider is angular and powerful. His hairstyle is affected in manner and crowned by a wreath of oak leaves.

Equally superb is the relief of the Mourning Athena, a work in the 'Severe Style' in which the goddess is represented wearing a Doric peplos and leaning on her spear, as she gazes pensively at a stele.

We proceed to the third storey of the museum and enter the Gallery of the Parthenon Sculptures. Here, the Parthenon frieze is incorporated in the rectangular concrete core of the museum, which is of the same dimensions as the cella of the Parthenon. With the metopes placed between the columns, the development of the figures on the two pediments and the uniting of authentic sculptures that escaped Elgin's predations with casts of those in the British Museum, we have for the first time the possibility of admiring the sculptural decoration of the Parthenon, with scenes of Gigantomachy, Centauromachy and Amazonomachy.

The most original and indeed unique sculptural decoration of the temple is the frieze, which represented the procession of the Panathenaia, the city's major festival. Of overall length 160 metres, it includes about 600 figures of gods, humans and animals. The greater part of it is in the British Museum and one mutilated block attests the cynicism of Elgin, whose agents used even a crowbar to detach the relief representation.

The last part of the exhibition is on the west and north sides of the Gallery

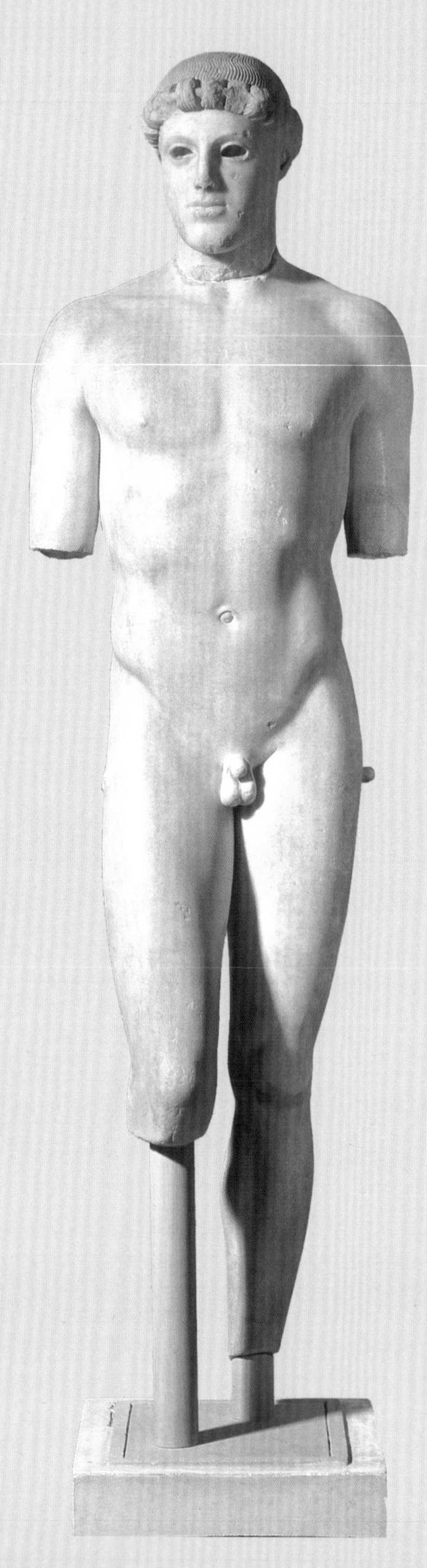

The Kritias Boy

of Archaic Works. Displayed here are the coffers from the roof of the Propylaia, the sculptures from the frieze and the parapet of the temple of Athena Nike, the sculptures from the frieze of the Erechtheion and, of course, five of the six authentic Karyatids from the south porch of the same temple.

The Blond Ephebe

ACROPOLIS MUSEUM
15 DIONYSIOU AREOPAGITOU ST
TEL.: 2109000901
TUESDAY - SUNDAY:
08.00-20.00 HRS
MONDAY: CLOSED

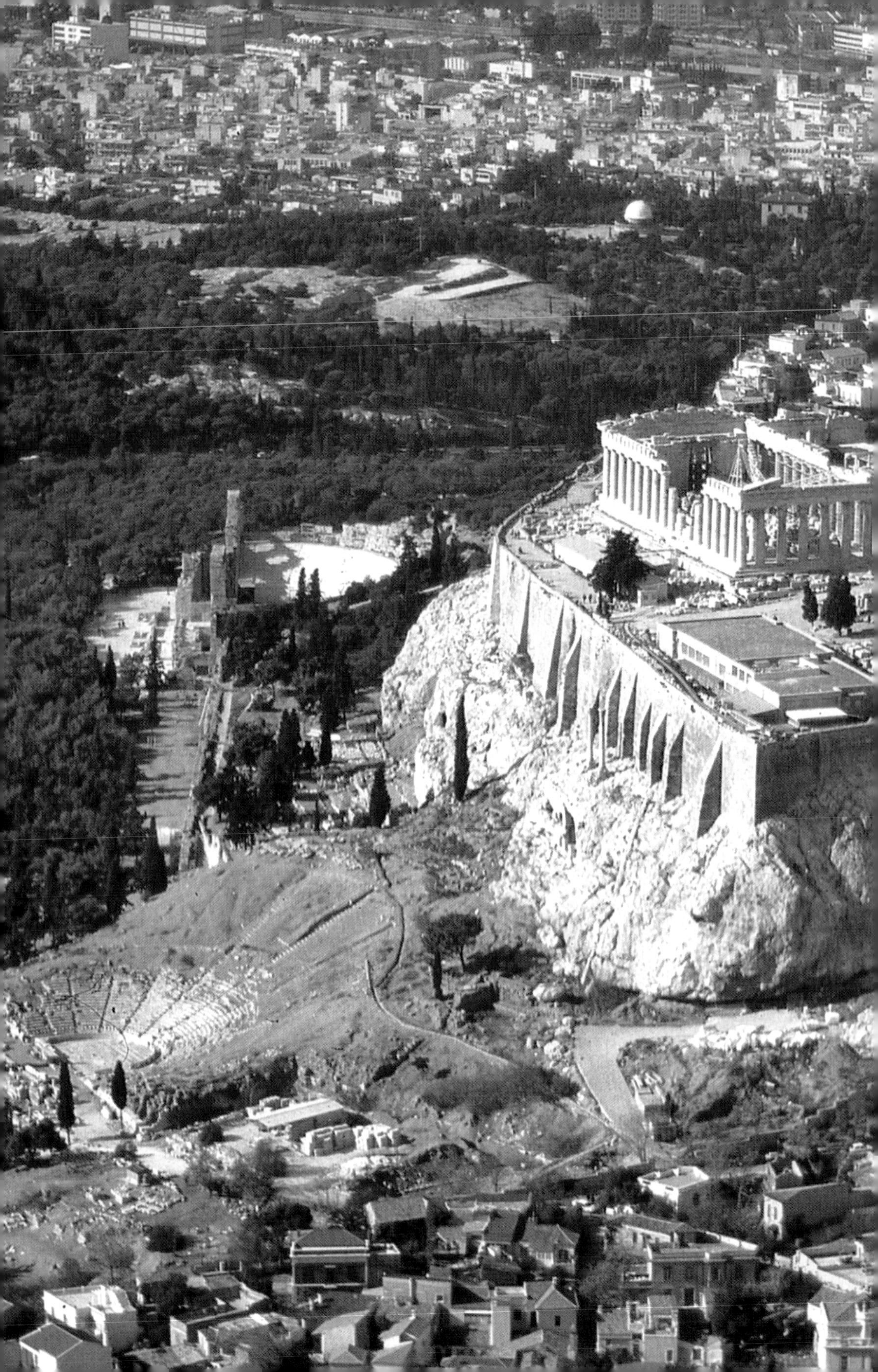

AROUND THE ROCK OF THE ACROPOLIS

THE THEATRE OF DIONYSOS

The theatre of Dionysos, the first theatre in history, was founded in the late sixth century BC. It was constructed with wooden seating and a simple wooden skene. At the centre was a rectangular *orchestra* (= 'dance place'), where the chorus danced around the altar to the god, the *thymele*. During the fifth century BC, the immortal plays by the tragic poets Aeschylus, Sophocles and Euripides, and the comic poet Aristophanes, were performed here.

In the fourth century BC, during the archonship of Lykourgos, the *cavea* (auditorium) was rebuilt of stone and acquired the form it has today, while the *skene* was altered many times in the ensuing centuries. The *cavea*, of maximum width 100 metres and depth 90 metres, includes 78 rows of seats, with an estimated capacity of 17,000 spectators. In the front row are 67 very elegant marble seats intended for the priests, officials and archons of the city. In the middle was the throne of the priest of Dionysos. In this phase of the theatre the orchestra became circular.

In Roman times, the theatre changed form twice, once in the reign of Emperor Nero and once in the archonship of Phaidros. The proscenium occupied part of the orchestra, which became semicircular, while the skene acquired a two-storey building (*scaenae frons*). Not long after, a parapet was constructed around the orchestra, in order to protect the spectators when gladiatorial duels and contests with wild beasts were held there. Moreover, the orchestra was frequently flooded with water and spectacles of mock naval battles were staged, with small-scale ship replicas. In the early fifth century AD a podium (bema) for speakers was installed in the orchestra. Known as the Bema of Phaidros, it was decorated with a lovely relief from an earlier monument.

THEATRE OF DIONYSOS
ENTRANCE FROM DIONYSIOU
AREOPAGITOU STREET
TEL.: 2103224625
OPEN DAILY: 08.00-20.00 HRS

Zeus, from the 'Bema of Phaidros'

Reliefs, on the 'Bema of Phaidros'

Marble seats in the front row *(prohedria)* of the theatre of Dionysos

THE SANCTUARY OF DIONYSOS

Dionysos was the god of vegetation, the vine and wine. His cult spread rapidly throughout Greece during the sixth century BC. It was introduced in Athens by Peisistratos, when the *xoanon* (wooden cult effigy) of the god was brought from the Boeotian city of Eleutherai and the Great Dionysia were organized, which were celebrated in the month of Elaphebolion (March-April). During this festival the men in the chorus dressed in goatskins and resembled satyrs. The ode sung by these men, who were called *tragoi* (= he-goats), was the seed from which tragedy sprouted. Preserved to the south of the theatre of Dionysos are remains of two temples, of the Archaic (6th century BC) and the Classical (4th century BC) period, which coexisted for many centuries.

Detail from a bronze statue of Dionysos

THE ODEION OF PERICLES

In the time of Pericles, the odeion named after him was built to the east of the cavea of the theatre of Dionysos. The Odeion of Pericles was used as a venue for music contests, and also as a law court. It was destroyed by fire in 86 BC, rebuilt in 61 BC and razed to the ground by the Heruls in AD 267.

Bust of Pericles

THE STOA OF EUMENES

Between the theatre of Dionysos and the Odeum of Herodes Atticus extends the Stoa of Eumenes II, king of Pergamon, which was built in the second century BC as a shelter for spectators in the event of bad weather, and as a place where Athenians could take a stroll and meet each other.

The stoa was 164 metres long, two-storeyed and had two colonnades, the external one with 64 Doric columns and the internal one with 32 Ionic columns. It was constructed of Hymettan marble and poros, and housed *ex-votos* and choregic monuments.

THE ASKLEPIEION

While the Peloponnesian War was in full swing and after the plague that decimated Athens, worship of the healing god Asklepios was introduced in the city. In 421/0 BC the Asklepieion was built, a sanctuary that hosted not only the temple and altar of the god, but also the *enkoimeterion*, a two-storey stoa that served as a dormitory in which the sick lodged, awaiting the help-cure of Asklepios. Ruins of the Asklepieion exist above the Stoa of Eumenes.

Statue of Asklepios

THE ODEUM OF HERODES ATTICUS

Tiberius Claudius Atticus Herodes was an extremely wealthy magnate and sophist, an Athenian citizen from the *demos* of Marathon, who lived in the second century AD. He was an orator and the mentor of many personalities of his day, served as eparch in Asia and was honoured in Athens with the office of chief priest of the Panathenaia. He inherited from his father a vast fortune, which he used for public-benefit works. Among his benefactions were the revetting of the Panathenaic Stadium with marble, the building of therapeutic bathing pools at Thermopylai, the Nymphaeum at Olympia and the Stadium at Delphi. In AD 161 he built the odeum in Athens, in memory of his wife Aspasia Annia Regilla. The Odeum of Herodes Atticus conforms to the type of Roman theatres. The *skene*, 35.40 metres long, is two-storeyed. The *orchestra* was 18.80 metres in diameter and paved with black and white tiles of marble from Karystos on the island of Euboea. The *cavea* comprises 32 rows and seats and can accommodate an audience of about 5,000.

The odeum was covered by a roof of cedar wood. The façade, a large part of which still stands, was grandiose in aspect, three-storeyed and with arched lintels. The odeum was destroyed by the Heruls in AD 267. It was restored in the decade 1950-1960 and every summer fills with spectators attending not only performances of ancient drama but also concerts, ballet and opera.

THE HILLS AROUND THE ACROPOLIS

Orestes killing his mother Clytemnestra. Representation from a bronze sheet

As soon as visitors have passed into the Acropolis and before reaching the Propylaia, they should pause awhile on a small terrace formed under the pedestal of Agrippa. From there they can look westwards, to the space in front of the sacred rock. At the base of the rock lie the ruins of the ancient Agora, the so-called Theseion and, a short distance to the west, the Areios Pagos.

The hill of the Areios Pagos or Areopagos was dedicated to the chthonic deities the Ares and later to the war god Ares. It was upon this rock that the first law court was founded and, according to Athenian tradition, it was here that Orestes was tried and condemned for the crime of murdering his mother Clytemnestra and her paramour Aegisthus, as immortalized in the *Oresteia* by Aeschylus. It was on this same historic hill that Paul the Apostle delivered his famous sermon about the ‘unknown god’, while the first Athenian to be baptized in the Christian faith was Dionysios the Areopagite, who became patron saint of Athens.

About 500 metres to the west of the Acropolis are three hills.

The first from the left, the Mouseion, was dedicated to the Nine Muses, patron divinities of the Arts and Sciences. It is known today as the Hill of Philopappus, because on its summit is the richly decorated mausoleum built by the Athenians in the second century AD to honour the Syrian benefactor of their city, the Roman ruler Gaius Julius Antiochus Philopappus.

The second hill is the Pnyx, the sacred space of the Ekklesia of the Demos (Citizens’ Assembly), the cradle of democracy, where for the first time in history citizens gained the right to vote. It was here that all male citizens over 30 years old assembled to debate and decide on the common weal, and it was here that the inspired speeches of Themistocles, Aristeides, Pericles and Demosthenes were heard.

Reconstruction of the monument of Philopappus

The third hill is that of the Nymphs, so named after the sanctuary of the Nymphs that existed here. In 1842, Baron Sinas founded the first Observatory of Athens on its summit. The plain building is of cruciform plan, with antennae at the four points of the compass, and has a large revolving dome at the centre.

Votive relief with dancing Nymphs

PLAKA

To the north and northeast of the Acropolis, at the foot of the rock, spreads the oldest neighbourhood in Athens, Plaka. In its picturesque narrow streets beats the heart of the old city. Monuments and remains of monuments of different periods coexist or are intermingled, giving a special charm and colour to this quarter, which has been inhabited continuously for the past six thousand years.

The monument of Lysikrates

LYSIKRATES SQUARE

To the northeast of the Theatre of Dionysos, in Lysikratous street in Plaka, is Lysikrates Square. At its centre stands an elegant ancient monument, popularly known as 'Diogenes' Lantern', which is in reality the choregic monument of Lysikrates. The *choregoi* were wealthy Athenian citizens who undertook to pay the expenses of the performances in the theatre of Dionysos and competed as to who could present the best. The victor was awarded a bronze or gilded tripod.

One such victorious *choregos* was Lysikrates, who in 334 BC built this monument in order to place at the top the tripod he had received as prize. The monument is over 9 metres high and consists of a square pedestal and a circular edifice (tholos). On the frieze are relief representations of the god Dionysos and at the top is the Corinthian column capital on which the tripod stood. The monument of Lysikrates is the best-preserved choregic monument in Athens.

ANAPHIOTIKA

At the foot of the north side of the Acropolis, in Plaka, is a settlement known as 'Anaphiotika'. It was named thus because its first inhabitants were from the Cycladic island of Anaphi. They came to Athens along with a host of other immigrants from the islands in 1840-1841, to work in the building trade in the new capital, which after its transfer from Nauplion was in the throes of a construction boom.

Many of these builders, and chiefly for economic reasons, built their houses without planning permission on this slope of the Acropolis. The settlement created is in layout and architecture reminiscent of the villages in the Cyclades.

Narrow streets in Plaka and detail of a Neoclassical house in the neighbourhood

THE OLD UNIVERSITY

In Upper Plaka, high on Tholou street, stands a very old residence, which from 1831 was the home of the architects Stamatis Kleanthis and Eduard Schaubert. In 1837 the first University of Athens began operating there. From the mid-nineteenth century and for many years, this building changed ownership and use several times. It was even turned into a taverna by the name of 'Palaio Panepistimio' (i.e. Old University). Today it is the University Museum.

BYZANTINE CHURCHES

With the prevailing of Christianity and the demise of the ancient pagan world, the star of Athens began slowly but steadily to wane. Both Emperor Theodosios II, who abolished the last sanctuaries still functioning in the fifth century AD, and Emperor Justinian, who closed the philosophical schools in the sixth century AD, dealt a mortal blow to the city of Pallas Athena. There is a dearth of information about Athens from the seventh to the ninth century. From the tenth to the twelfth century the city seems to have flourished a little.

Constantinople began to take an interest in Athens and so clerics and artists came here, building a host of small but very lovely churches.

There are numerous Byzantine churches in the neighbourhood of Plaka, in the narrow streets between the houses. Among the oldest is the little church of the Transfiguration of the Saviour in Theorias street, at the north foot of the Acropolis, which is dated to the second half of the eleventh century. At the junction of Erechtheos and Erotokritou streets stands the church of St John the Theologian, which is a twelfth-century building and survives in good condition. A short distance beyond, in Prytaneiou street, is St Nicholas Rangavas, a typical Byzantine church of the eleventh-twelfth century, to which several additions were made in 1977-1978.

Close to the monument of Lysikrates is the church of St Catherine, a dependency (*metochi*) of the homonymous monastery on Mount Sinai. It was built in the eleventh-twelfth century on the site of an Early Christian basilica, remnants of which can be seen in its courtyard. Repairs and additions made in later times have considerably altered its original aspect. Another surviving Byzantine church, one of the earliest in Athens, is that of the Saviour of Kottakis, at the corner of Kydathinaion and Sotiros streets. It was built around the end of the tenth century and it is probably that the eponym 'of Kottakis' is due to the founders, members of a known Athenian family.

The church of St Nicholas Rangavas

THE CANELLOPOULOS MUSEUM

An imposing Neoclassical mansion in Plaka, below the rock of the Acropolis, houses the Paul and Alexandra Canellopoulos Museum, which presents works from the private collection donated by the couple to the Greek State in 1972.

About 6,000 objects and artworks are exhibited, spanning the Neolithic to the Modern Age and classified in chronological units. Vases, weapons, jewellery, figurines, sculptures, sealstones and grave stelai attest to the wide scope of Greek creation from prehistoric into recent times.

Chronologically, the works begin from the Neolithic Age (6800-3200 BC) and the Bronze Age (3200-1100 BC), covering the Cycladic Culture, the Minoan and the Mycenaean Civilization, and continue in historical times with the Geometric (900-700 BC), the Archaic (7th- 6th century BC), Classical (5th-4th century BC), Hellenistic (3rd-2nd century BC) and Roman periods, as well as the Byzantine Age and the Post-Byzantine period.

Impressive is the unit of '*Tanagraies*', delightful little female figurines in terracotta from Tanagra in Boeotia. Dating from the fourth and third centuries BC, these elegant figures have elaborate hats, garments and hairstyles. Important too is the collection of 270 icons, most of them Post-Byzantine, among which are signed works by significant artists, such as Michael Damaskenos, a notable painter of the Cretan School in the sixteenth century.

CANELLOPOULOS MUSEUM
12 PANOS & THEORIAS ST - PLAKA
TEL.: 2103212313
TUESDAY - SUNDAY:
08.30-15.00 HRS
MONDAY: CLOSED

THE MUSEUM OF GREEK FOLK ART

The Museum of Greek Folk Art was founded in 1918, under the name of the Museum of Greek Handicrafts. It was renamed the National Museum of Decorative Arts in 1923, and in 1959 took the name by which it is known today.

It was housed originally in the Jistaraki Mosque in Monastiraki Square, and was moved to the premises in Kydathinaion Street in 1973. Presented in the three storeys of the museum is the development of Greek folk art from the period of its heyday into modern times, spanning some one hundred and fifty years.

Exhibits included embroideries that are true masterpieces, from all regions of Greece, wood-carvings, jewellery, weapons and ecclesiastical vessels, as well as a large number of local costumes, male and female, for everyday and festive wear.

MUSEUM OF GREEK FOLK ART
17 KYDATHINAION ST - PLAKA
TEL.: 2103229031
TUESDAY - SUNDAY:
10 .00-14.00 HRS
MONDAY: CLOSED

THE CENTRE OF GREEK FOLK ART AND TRADITION

The Centre of Greek Folk Art and Tradition was founded in 1980 and is housed in the former residence of Greek folklorist Angeliki Hadjimichali, in the street named after her.

Angeliki Hadjimichali was born in Plaka in 1895 and died in 1966. She travelled throughout Greece and wrote several studies on the country's folk culture. Her most important work is on the Sarakatsani, a transhumant Greek population that was virtually unknown until then. She also founded the Association of Greek Handicraft.

Displayed are collections of significant works of folk art, such as textiles and embroideries, wood-carvings, vessels and vases. The centre also has a very rich library.

CENTRE OF GREEK FOLK ART AND TRADITION
6 ANGELIKI HADJIMICHALI ST - PLAKA
TEL.: 21032439871
TUESDAY - FRIDAY: 9 .00-13.00, 17.00-21.00 HRS
SATURDAY - SUNDAY: 9.00-13.00 HRS
MONDAY: CLOSED

THE MUSEUM OF GREEK FOLK MUSICAL INSTRUMENTS

The mansion of freedom-fighter Georgios Lassanis, which was built in 1842, close to the Roman Agora, today houses the Museum of Greek Folk Musical Instruments. Exhibited are musical instruments from the collection of the musicologist Foivos Anoyannakis, which he donated to the Greek State in 1978. Visitors to the museum have the opportunity not only of seeing these instruments, which date from the eighteenth century, but also of hearing the sounds of clarinets (*klarina*), shawms (*zournades*), *lyres*, *baglamades*, children's whistles, shells and others.

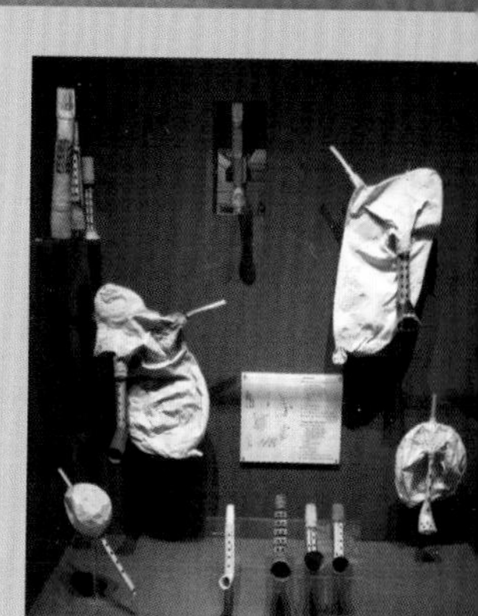

MUSEUM OF GREEK FOLK MUSICAL INSTRUMENTS
1 DIOGENOUS ST - PLAKA
TEL.: 2103254119
TUESDAY, THURSDAY - SUNDAY: 10 .00-14.00 HRS
WEDNESDAY: 12.00-18.00 HRS
MONDAY: CLOSED

THE AERIDES BATHHOUSE

The only surviving *hamam* (public bathhouse) in Athens is in Plaka. The *hamam* of Abid Efendi, popularly known as the '*Loutro ton Aeridon*' (Aerides Bathhouse), operated regularly until 1965. In 1984 it became the property of the Museum of Greek Folk Art and in 1998 works on its restoration were completed. Visitors can see the series of chambers of the *hamam*, starting from the changing rooms, where bathers waited and were entertained. They then passed to the tepid chamber, where the body began gradually to become acclimatized to the heat, and from there into the third chamber, which was very hot and is equipped with basins with running water. There were separate facilities for men and for women, as well as for use by both.

THE AREA OF THE ANCIENT AGORA

The Greek word *agora* is derived from the verb *ageiro*, which means to assemble, to congregate. In Antiquity the agora was not only the venue for commercial transactions, but also the space where citizens met and mingled to learn and discuss the latest news, since there were no mass media of communication.

THE ANCIENT AGORA

Between the hills of Agoraios Kolonos and the Areos Pagos lies the site of the ancient Agora, which was the heart of the civic life of Athens. Of irregular quadrilateral shape, it is delimited by stoas and rows of buildings, and through it runs diagonally the Panathenaic Way, the street along which the Panathenaia procession passed. All public services, government buildings, public sanctuaries and statues of mythical and historical persons were concentrated there.

Dominating the site of the ancient Agora is the temple of Hephaistos, the so-called Theseion, which stands on the hill of Agoraios Kolonos. The very good state of preservation of this edifice is due to the fact that it was converted into a Christian church. Although of smaller dimensions than the Parthenon, it vies with it in beauty and architectural perfection. From early on this temple and its environs were named Theseion, but it is now known that the temple was dedicated to Hephaistos and Athena, and that their cult statues, works of the sculptor Alkamenes, were in its cella.

The Hephaistion was built just after the mid-fifth century BC. It is in the Doric order with 6 x 13 columns. The cella is amphiprostyle *in antis* and has a pronaos and an opisthodomos. The columns have slight *entasis* and incline slightly towards the centre. Represented on the metopes are the Labours of Herakles and of Theseus, while represented on the inside frieze are Centauromachy and the Battle between Theseus and the Pallantids, claimants to the throne of Athens. After the prevailing of Christianity, the temple was turned into a church as we have said dedicated to St George, who was venerated there until 1834, when the Hephaistion it was declared a national monument.

The temple of Hephaistos, the so-called 'Theseion'

Visible on the west side of the Agora and at the foot of the Agoraios Kolonos hill are the foundations of a circular building, the Tholos, which was the seat of the administration of the city-state. Inside the Tholos the 50 serving *prytaneis*, that is, one-tenth of the *bouleutai*, ate their meals. Some of them stayed there continuously during their term of service. It was built *circa* 470 BC, to replace an earlier edifice that had been destroyed by the Persians.

Reconstruction of the Tholos, in the Agora

North of the Tholos was the New Bouleuterion (Council Hall), which was built in the late fifth century BC to the west of the first bouleuterion. There the Boule (Council of Deputies) of Five Hundred met in session after the Peloponnesian War. East of the bouleuterion are the foundations of the Metroon, which housed the sanctuary of the Mother of the Gods, Rhea, and the archives of the State.

In front of these buildings stood a high marble pedestal, which held bronze statues of the Ten Eponymous Heroes, after whom the ten tribes of Attica were named. On the front of the pedestal were wooden notice boards on which were hung public announcements, official proclamations, military recruitment commands, amendments to legislation, and so on.

A short distance beyond the Metroon are the foundations of a small temple of the fourth century BC, which was dedicated to Apollo Patroos, father of Ion, founding ancestor of the Ionians. Adjacent to the temple was a Π-shaped stoa in which Zeus Eleutherios was worshipped, as god of freedom.

In the same row, just past the railway track, is the Royal Stoa (Stoa Basileios), seat of the Archon Basileus, the magistrate who presided over the council of the Areopagos, which met there. To the north of Adrianou street was the Painted Stoa (Poikile Stoa), constructed under Kimon around 460 BC and decorated with wall-paintings. It was known as a meeting place for philosophers.

Situated in front of the stoa of Zeus Eleutherios was the temple of Ares, constructed in the fifth century BC. To the north of it was the Altar of the Twelve Gods and to the south the Odeum erected by M.V. Agrippa in the first century BC, which could accommodate an audience of 1,000. In the early fifth century AD, the odeum was incorporated into an enormous building which was probably a commandery or residence of the Byzantine empress Eudokia, who originated from Athens and was wife of Emperor Theodosius II the Younger. The colossal statues of one Giant and two Tritons, which we see today and which adorned the propylon of the building, belonged previously to the odeum.

On the south side of the Agora there were three stoas the Middle, the East and the South to the west of which was located either the most important Attic law court, the Heliaia, or, according to a more recent view, the Aiakeion sanctuary. Along the east side of the Agora runs the Stoa of Attalos.

THE MUSEUM OF THE ANCIENT AGORA

On the east side of the Agora is the Stoa of Attalos, constructed by Attalos II, king of Pergamon, in the second century BC. Today fully restored, this two-storey construction, 116.50 metres long and 19.50 metres wide, is fronted by a double colonnade.

In Antiquity it functioned as a 'shopping mall', with a row of 21 shops on each storey. Today it houses the small Museum of the Ancient Agora and storerooms for finds from the Agora excavations.

Displayed in the museum are unique objects associated with the functioning of the democracy in Athens. Some of the most significant exhibits are the statue of Apollo Patroos, work of the sculptor Euphranor, of the fourth century BC, and a statue of Aphrodite, of the same period. Outstanding too are the 'Iliad' and the 'Odyssey', statues of the second century AD, a bronze head of Nike, diverse clay vases from the sixth century BC to the sixth century AD, and an ivory pyxis of *ca* 1400 BC.

Also exhibited in the Agora museum are artefacts relating to daily life, such as coins, rattles, toys and a considerable number of *ostraka*. The last are potsherds on which the Athenians incised the name of anyone they considered a danger to the democracy. A ballot was held and the person named the most times was banished from the city for ten years; this procedure is known as ostracism.

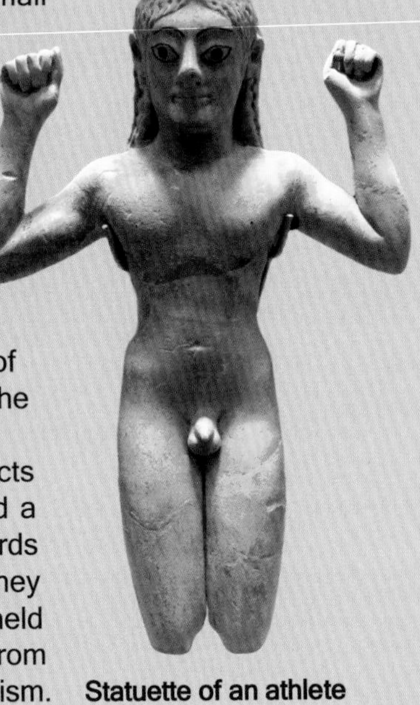

Statuette of an athlete

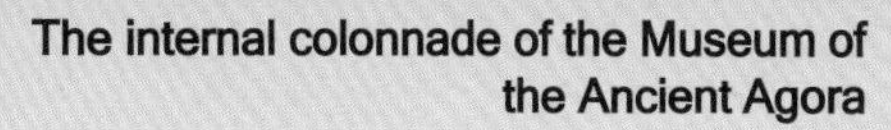

The internal colonnade of the Museum of the Ancient Agora

ANCIENT AGORA - MUSEUM OF THE ANCIENT AGORA
TEL.: 2103210185
TUESDAY - SUNDAY:
8.30-15.00 HRS
MONDAY: CLOSED

Bronze head of a Nike

THE ROMAN AGORA

Reconstruction of the Roman Agora

Next to the Stoa of Attalos ran a street that led to a second agora, the Roman. The Roman Agora or Agora of Caesar and Augustus was built in the late first century BC and was purely commercial in character. It is a large space enclosed by a colonnade in the Ionic order, while it is suspected that there was an internal Doric colonnade as well on the north and south sides. The building materials used are marble from Hymettos and Pentele, and poros from Piraeus.

On the east side of the Roman Agora there were several buildings of the first century AD, such as the Agoranomeion (headquarters of the market inspectors), the public latrines and the Vespasians, traces of which were uncovered in the 1930s, when systematic excavations of the site began.

ROMAN AGORA
1 AIOLOU ST - PLAKA
TEL.: 2103245220
TUESDAY - SUNDAY:
8.30-15.00 HRS
MONDAY: CLOSED

Preserved on the west side of the Roman Agora is a propylon in the Doric order, known as the Gate of Athena Archegetis. During the period of Ottoman rule, farmers and merchants coming to Athens to sell their wares in the bazaars (*pazaria*) congregated around this gateway, which was thus known popularly as the Pazaroporta.

THE HOROLOGION OF ANDRONIKOS KYRRHESTOS

On the east side of the Roman Agora stands the best-preserved monument in this area, the Horologion ('clock') built in the first century AD by the astronomer Andronikos from Kyrrhe, upon a three-stepped crepis of Pentelic marble. At the top of each side of this octagonal tower are reliefs with personifications of the winds, and below these, again on each side, was a sundial.

The monument is known also as the Tower of the Winds or Aerides, because of the relief representations.

At the apex of the conical marble roof there was a weathervane in the form of a Triton, whose staff pointed the direction of the prevailing wind. The Horologion operated as both a sundial and a hydraulic clock of the agora, powered by water descending from the Acropolis.

Boreas and Zephyros, from the Clock-Tower of Andronikos Kyrrhestos

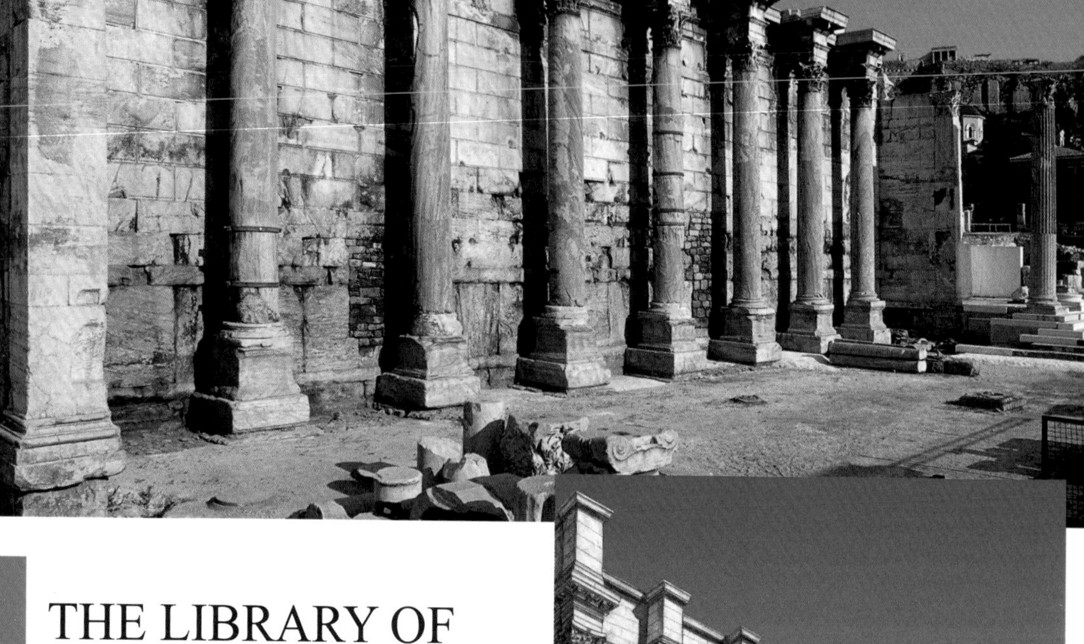

THE LIBRARY OF HADRIAN

To the north of the Roman Agora is the huge building of the second century AD known as the Library of Hadrian. Of rectangular plan (122 x 28 metres) and with a large internal court, the monument included lecture halls, a library, a theatre and a spacious garden with cistern.

Reconstruction of the Library of Hadrian

The court was surrounded by a peristyle of 100 columns of Phrygian marble, which accommodated porticoes some 750 metres deep. The walls of the porticoes were of poros, excepting the entrance to the Library, where there is isodomic masonry of Pentelic marble. The propylon at the entrance is tetrastyle in the Corinthian order and is flanked by two Corinthian colonnades with monolithic smooth-shafted columns.

The Library was badly damaged by the Heruls in AD 267. Around the beginning of the fifth century AD, another building, with four apses, was constructed, which was destroyed in the sixth century AD. Built upon its ruins was a three-aisle basilica, which in the eleventh century was replaced by a little Byzantine church.

MONASTIRAKI

Monastiraki, the neighbourhood of Athens around Monastiraki Square, is located at one of the most distinctive points in the city centre. It takes its name from the monastery (Gr. diminutive *monastiraki*) that existed here in the seventeenth century and for many years supplied the market with cloth woven by the monks. This stood on the north side of the present square, where the church of the Virgin Panatanassa stands today.

On the opposite side of Monastiraki Square is the Jistaraki mosque, one of the five Muslim places of worship that existed in Athens in Ottoman times. It was built in 1759 by the Turkish voevod or governor of the city and for its construction the Turks pulled down one column of the Olympieion. This was considered such a heinous act of vandalism that Athenians associated it with the plague epidemic which struck the city in the same year.

For hundreds of years Monastiraki Square was the commercial hub of Athens. The streets around it were home to many shops selling cloth and ribbons, to tanneries and smithies. Over time, all these activities moved to streets further away from the square, giving way to shops selling folk-art items, souvenirs and antiques. The square is at its liveliest on Sundays, when the open-air flea market attracts crowds of people.

REECE

THE METROPOLIS

(GREEK ORTHODOX CATHEDRAL)

The Metropolis or Greek Orthodox Cathedral of Athens is situated in Metropolis Square in Mitropoleos street, a main thoroughfare of the city.

The foundation stone was laid in 1842 and the church was completed in 1862. The original plans were by the Danish architect Theophilus Hansen and included Gothic and Romanesque elements, but as work progressed these were modified by the architects D. Zezos and F. Boulanger, who designed a three-aisle basilica with dome. There is information that the cathedral was constructed of material from 70 demolished churches. The Metropolis is dedicated to the Annunciation to the Virgin.

THE CHURCH OF THE VIRGIN GORGOEPEKOOS

Next to the Metropolis stands the most original of all the Byzantine churches of Athens, known as the Little Metropolis or the Virgin Gorgoepekoos (the Swift-hearing) or St Eleutherios. Built in the twelfth century, the church is of cruciform plan with dome, but differs from traditional churches in the material used for its construction. The architect gathered remains of monuments from almost all historical periods and used these *spolia* with unique skill and imagination to create a harmonious edifice distinguished by elegance and charm.

Incorporated in the walls are reliefs with representations of humans and vases, friezes with triglyphs, ancient and Byzantine stelai with decorative motifs, and metopes. On the façade are Corinthian column capitals and Byzantine carvings. Represented on the epistyle are two lions flanking a cross, and a little way above is an ancient frieze presenting the Attic calendar. Various symbols from the zodiac cycle indicate the months, and scenes depict their principal festivals.

Many of the silver votive offerings (*tamata*) placed on the icon of St Eleutherios represent babies, because this saint, who was believed to ensure easy childbirth, replaced the ancient goddess of childbirth, Eileithyia.

THE CHURCH OF KAPNIKAREA

At the intersection of Ermou and Aiolou streets stands the eleventh-century Byzantine church known as Kapnikarea. Dedicated to the Virgin, its name is taken from the occupation or the name of the founder, Kapnikaris, or from the *kamouchades*, who produced and sold luxurious textiles in this quarter. The church is of cruciform plan with a dome supported on four columns. Its exterior is particularly lovely and interesting, with careful masonry in which many ancient architectural members (*spolia*) are incorporated.

THE CHURCH OF THE INCORPOREAL SAINTS (HAGIOI ASOMATOI)

Continuing down Ermou street, from Kapnikarea, in the direction of the Kerameikos, we come to a small Byzantine church next to the Theseion station of the urban railway. Dedicated to the Incorporeal Saints (Hagioi Asomatoi), it stands at the centre of Agion Asomaton Square. Although built in the eleventh century, its present aspect is very close to the original, after restoration works carried out in the 1960s, which relieved it of additions and interventions made over the centuries. It is a typical church of the Byzantine period, that is, of cruciform plan, four-columned and with dome.

THE KERAMEIKOS

Two neighbourhoods of ancient Athens, located on its northwest side and belonging to the *demos* of Kerameoi of the Akamantis tribe, are known by the name Kerameikos: Exo (Outer) Kerameikos, which was *extra muros*, and Eso (Inner) Kerameikos, which was *intra muros*. The name Kerameikos derives from the workshops of potters (Gr. *keramoi*), which abounded in the area. The two neighbourhoods communicated via the Dipylon, the main entrance to Athens. As its name indicates, the Dipylon consisted of two gateways, which were protected by two towers, on the west and the east side respectively. The court thus formed was closed from all directions and so trapped any enemy trying to enter the city.

The Dipylon was the starting point for the roads leading from Athens to the Piraeus and to the Academy of Plato, while from the inside runs the Panathenaic Way that passed through the Agora and terminated at the Acropolis. Southwest of the Dipylon there was one other gateway,

called the Hiera (Sacred) Pyle because from here passed the procession of the Eleusinian Mysteries, on its way to Eleusis. Between the Dipylon and the Hiera Pyle stood the so-called Pompeion, a building complex in which preparations for the major festivals took place.Over the years, Exo Kerameikos was transformed into the main cemetery of ancient Athens, because the Athenians were accustomed to burying their dead outside the walls of the city. The most important part of the cemetery was the road leading to the Academy where Plato taught. This road was lined by monuments of eminent Athenians and mass graves of Athenians who fell in battle for the honour and glory of their city. It was here that Pericles delivered his Funerary Oration for the dead in the Peloponnesian War, and that the funerary orations of Demosthenes and Hypereides were heard. Among the illustrious Athenians buried in the Kerameikos were Kleisthenes, Thrasyboulos, the tyrannicides Harmodios and Aristogeiton, Lykourgos and Pericles.

Impressive and well-preserved is the part of the cemetery in which there are private tombs. Wonderful funerary monuments adorning these attest to the Athenians' good taste and respect of the dead. Notable are the tomb of Dexileos, decorated with a relief in which he is represented on horseback slaying his adversary, and the tomb of Dionysios, with the statue of a bull.

The tomb of Dionysios

THE KERAMEIKOS MUSEUM

The exhibits in this small but impressive museum come chiefly from the Kerameikos cemetery. They include various grave stelai of the Archaic period. Outstanding are the stelai of Dexileos and of Ampharete. Interesting too are the funerary vases, which date from the Mycenaean to the Roman period and include enormous Geometric amphorae and white lekythoi.

KERAMEIKOS
KERAMEIKOS MUSEUM
148 ERMOU ST, TEL.: 2103463552
TUESDAY - SUNDAY:
8.30-15.00 HRS
MONDAY: CLOSED

The grave stele of Dexileos

THE AREA OF THE OLYMPIEION

The area of the sanctuary of Zeus Olympios or the Olympieion is full of memories of myth and history. Archaeological finds and the ancient sources attest that it was inhabited from very early times. The River Ilissos flowed through here and the Athenians believed that it was here that the final waters from Deukalion's flood receded. Indeed, Deukalion was said to have built at the point where they disappeared an altar dedicated to Zeus. The area was home to the Kallirrhoe spring and the cave of the Nymphs, and somewhere hereabouts Boreas seized Erecththeus' daughter, Oreithyia, as she was picking flowers on the river banks. In the shade of a plane tree close to the spring, Socrates discoursed with his disciples.

THE OLYMPIEION

The temple of Zeus Olympios, the largest ancient temple in Athens, is built in an open space over 200 metres long and 130 metres wide. Construction commenced in the time of Peisistratos, in the sixth century BC, but this first poros temple with enormous columns was never finished.

In 175 BC, Antiochos Epiphanes commissioned the Roman architect Cossutius to change the plans of the temple, in an effort to continue the project. Cossutius designed columns in the Corinthian order, of Pentelic marble, but again works stopped on the death of Antiochos. Building of the temple was finally completed, on the orders of

Reconstruction of the temple of Zeus Olympios (Olympieion)

Emperor Hadrian, in AD 132, seven centuries after works began.

The temple is in the Doric order, dipteral, with two rows of 20 columns on the long sides, and 8 columns on the two fronts. Only 16 of the 104 gigantic columns, 17.25 metres high, survive. The temple housed a chryselephantine statue of Zeus and one other statue portraying Hadrian.

MONUMENTS IN THE AREA OF THE OLYMPIEION

To the north of the temple is an earlier peripteral temple in the Doric order, of 500 BC, which was dedicated to Apollo Delphinios, and to the west is a building with large court and many rooms, the 'Law Court by the Delphinion'. Finds from south of the Olympieion indicate that the temple of Apollo Pythios stood there. To the northwest were the Sanctuary of Gaia and the Sanctuary of Aphrodite '*en Kepois*' (= in the gardens) and of Artemis Agrotera (= of the fields).

The temple of Zeus Panhellenios, dedicated to Hadrian, Zeus and Hera, a *balneum* (bathhouse) and a small Doric temple dedicated to Kronos and Rhea date from the Roman period.

OLYMPIEION AND SANCTUARIES ON THE BANKS OF THE ILISSOS
1. VAS. OLGAS ST - ZAPPEION
TEL.: 2109226330
DAILY: 08.00-20.00 HRS

THE ARCH OF HADRIAN

In AD 131, the Athenians erected the Arch of Hadrian, just beyond the Olympieion, in order to honour the great benefactor of their city. This arch or gateway separated the neighbourhoods that developed around the Olympieion, which were named the New City or City of Hadrian, from the Old City of Athens. The Arch of Hadrian is 18 metres high and is constructed of Pentelic marble. It comprises an arched gateway, on top of which is a row of Corinthian columns, the two middle ones of which are crowned by a small pediment. On the narrow frieze, on the east face above the arch, is an inscription that reads in translation: 'This is the city of Hadrian and not of Theseus'. On the west side there is another inscription, which reads: 'This is Athens, the old city of Theseus'.

THE ZAPPEION

The Zappeion Megaron stands in a public park which is an extension of the National Garden. A Neoclassical building, one of the largest in area in this style in Athens, it has a semicircular plan, an internal court and a monumental entrance in the Corinthian order. Construction began in 1874 and was completed in 1888. The project was financed by the Zappas brothers, whose statues stand on either side of the entrance to the megaron. The initial plans were drawn by the French architect François-Louis-Florimond Boulanger, but the final form was designed by the Danish architect Theophilus Hansen.

The Zappeion Megaron was intended as a venue for exhibitions, international conferences, scientific meetings and other social events. In May 1979, the accession of Greece to the then European Economic Community was signed in the Zappeion hall.

THE NATIONAL GARDEN

The National Garden lies behind the Zappeion and occupies an area of 16 hectares. The first designs for its layout were prepared in 1836 by the architect of the Old Palace of King Othon, now the House of Parliament. However, in 1839, by decision of Queen Amalia, the garden was redesigned from scratch by another architect and named the Royal Garden. It took ten years to arrange and plant, and until 1854 was for the exclusive use of the royal family.

In 1923 it was renamed the National Garden and became a public park open to all. It has been a favourite place for Athenians to stroll and relax ever since.

The garden has many lofty trees and countless plants, duck ponds, a children's playground, a small zoo and a small botanical museum. The trees and plants are representative not only of the flora of Greece but also of subtropical regions.

NATIONAL GARDEN
DAILY: 08.00 - TO SUNSET

THE PRESIDENTIAL PALACE

The Presidential Palace stands in Irodou Attikou street and was designed by architect Ernst Ziller. Building commenced in 1891 and finished in 1897. This was the new palace of the royal family from 1910 until 1974 and the restoration of democracy after the military dictatorship (1967-1974). Since 1974 the palace serves as the official residence of the President of the Hellenic Republic and is guarded by the Euzones, soldiers in traditional Greek costume.

THE RUSSIAN CHURCH

The Russian church, also known as the Saviour of Lykodemos, is one of the two churches of octagon type that survive in Athens and its environs. It was built in the early eleventh century. The dome covers the entire nave and the masonry on the outside is richly decorated with sun, cross and other motifs.

The church suffered severe damage in 1687, during the siege of Athens by Morosini, and in 1701 from an earthquake. In 1852 it was ceded to the Russians, who restored it and built the bell-tower. Today it is the place of worship of the Russian Orthodox community in Athens.

THE PANATHENAIC STADIUM

A short distance from the Olympieion, on the left bank of the River Ilissos, is the Panathenaic Stadium, also known as the Kallimarmaro (because it is revetted in marble). One of the most impressive monuments in Athens, it was constructed initially in the fourth century BC, under the supervision of the orator Lykourgos. The athletics contests associated with the Panathenaia festival were held here. That stadium had wooden seats for the archons, while the spectators sat on the sloping ground.

The stadium was rebuilt by Herodes Atticus in the second century AD. Much larger and with marble seats, it could accommodate 50,000 people. It fell into ruins during the dark years of the Ottoman period. In the late nineteenth century, the benefactor of the Nation, Georgios Averoff, revetted the stadium once again in marble, in order for it to host the first modern Olympic Games, in 1896.

PANATHENAIC STADIUM
DAILY: 08.00 - SUNSET

THE FIRST CEMETERY

To the south of the Stadium is the First Cemetery of Athens. According to a document referring to the building of a wall around it, the cemetery was already in use from 1837. In 1842 the regulations of its operation were drafted and in the period 1857-1861 pathways were laid and trees planted.

The church of Sts Theodore stands at the entrance, from where begin the various sectors into which the cemetery is divided: the sector with the oldest tombs, the Catholic sector, the Protestant sector, and so on.

In the First Cemetery are the tombs of leading freedom-fighters in the 1821 War of Independence, such as Makrygiannis, and of eminent politicians, such as Charilaos Trikoupos and Georgios Papandreou, of intellectual figures, such as Adamantios Korais and George Seferis. On many tomb monuments in the cemetery there are works of art that recall those of Antiquity, such as sarcophagi, funerary lekythoi, grave stelai, small funerary temples, as well as gravestones with flowers and full-bodied figures in relief.

One of the most important monuments in the First Cemetery, or rather a Modern Greek work of art, is the 'Sleeping Maiden', created by the sculptor Giannoulis Chalepas in 1878. This figure, which appears to be resting in deep slumber, presenting death as the eternal sleep, marks the tomb of Sophia Afentaki.

The First Cemetery is a veritable source of study for the recent history of Athens and the burial customs of the Greeks, and a great open-air museum of Modern Greek sculpture.

FIRST CEMETERY
DAILY: 08.00 - SUNSET

The ‘Sleeping Maiden’ by Chalepas

THE AREA OF SYNTAGMA SQUARE

The Greek House of Parliament, many public buildings, big luxury hotels and Syntagma (Constitution) Square itself compose the space where the heart of Athens beats. The area of Syntagma Square is the centre of the political life of the whole of Greece.

THE HOUSE OF PARLIAMENT

The building that houses the Greek Parliament was built in the period 1836-1842 to plans by the Bavarian architect Friedrich von Gärtner. For almost one hundred years it served as the palace of kings Othon and George I. In 1910, after a fire that destroyed the interior, the royal family moved to the New Palace, which is today the Presidential Palace. Since 1931, and following restoration works and changes to the interior, the Old Palace has housed the Greek Parliament. In front of the House of Parliament is the monument to the Unknown Soldier, which was built in 1932 to plans by architect Emmanuel Lazaridis and the sculptor Phokion Rok.

This is a cenotaph that was created to commemorate the war dead. Represented in relief is a naked soldier with only his weapons, flanked by carved excerpts from the Funeral Oration of Pericles, as narrated by Thucydides, and names of regions where the Greek Army has fought in recent times. The memorial is guarded continuously by Euzones, who wear the traditional Greek costume known as *foustanella*.

SYNTAGMA SQUARE

Opposite the monument to the Unknown Soldier is Syntagma (Constitution) Square. The best-known square in Athens, it was originally called Palace Square, but after the events of 3 September 1843, when the Athenians held a mass rally demanding that King Othon grant a constitution, it was renamed Syntagma Square.

The square is surrounded by several traditional coffee shops and buildings of considerable architectural interest. The most important of the latter, on its north side, was constructed in 1842 to plans by Theophilus Hansen. At first an opulent mansion, in 1872 it was converted into the Grande Bretagne Hotel.

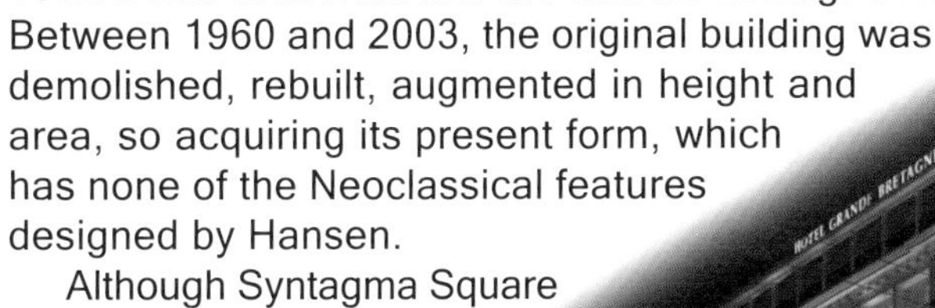

Between 1960 and 2003, the original building was demolished, rebuilt, augmented in height and area, so acquiring its present form, which has none of the Neoclassical features designed by Hansen.

Although Syntagma Square has been remodelled many times in recent years, it has never ceased to be the centre of the political and social life of Athens.

THE BENAKI MUSEUM

The Benaki Museum is located opposite the National Garden, in a Neoclassical mansion of 1900, on Vasilissis Sophias Avenue. The grand residence with its marble Doric columns and marble balconies was designed by architect Anastasios Metaxas and was purchased by Emmanuel Benakis in 1910.

His son, Antonios Benakis (1837-1954), an expatriate businessman in Egypt, was a connoisseur and an avid collector of works of art. When he came to settle permanently in Athens, in 1927, he decided to found a museum to house his collection and to donate it to the Greek State. Thus, in 1931, the museum was inaugurated in his magnificent Neoclassical parental home. Over the years the museum expanded, the spaces were arranged according to the collections they hosted, with the result that visitors today can admire over 35,000 exhibits.

Displayed in the museum are Greek works of art from prehistoric times to the Modern Age. Palaeolithic and Neolithic artefacts from various regions of Greece and Cyprus, objects of the Cycladic Culture and the Minoan and Mycenaean civilizations, vases of the Archaic period, jewellery, pottery and sculpture of the fifth and fourth centuries BC, works of the Hellenistic and Roman eras, silverwork, embroideries, wood-carvings, Byzantine and Post-Byzantine icons, weapons of the 1821 freedom-fighters, are some of the categories of exhibits in the museum’s possession.

So intensive is the activity of the Benaki Museum that it has established annexes

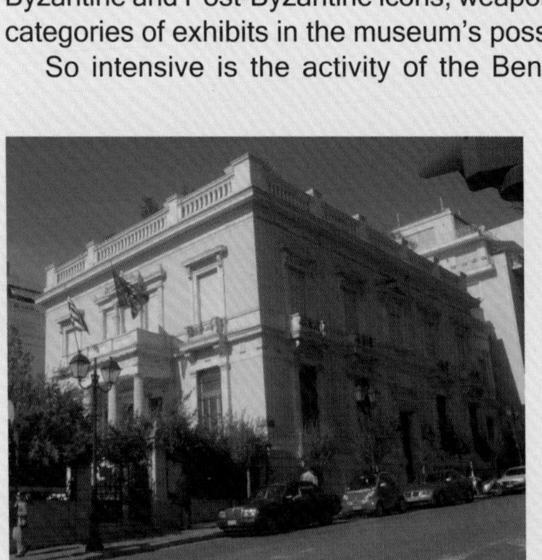

elsewhere in the city: in Kerameikos (Museum of Islamic Art), Kiphissia (Historical Archives Department), Kolonaki (Hadjikyriakos-Ghikas Gallery) and, last, a new exhibition space in the Gazi neighbourhood.

BENAKI MUSEUM
1 KOUMBARI ST - ATHENS
TEL.: 2103671000

THE MUSEUM OF CYCLADIC ART

The main building of the Museum of Cycladic Art, in Neophytou Douka street in Kolonaki, was inaugurated in 1986 by the N.P. Goulandris Foundation, to house the Collection of Cycladic and Ancient Greek Art formed by Nikolaos and Dolly Goulandris, as well as to promote the culture of the Aegean and the prehistoric Cyclades. In 1991 the museum expanded into premises at the corner of Vasilissis Sophias Avenue and Irodotou street, the former Stathatos Mansion.

Exhibited on the four floors of the main building are the Cycladic Collection, the most complete private collection in the world, of some 350 pieces.

The Collection of Ancient Greek Art (2000 BC - 4th century AD); the Thanos Zintilis Collection of Cypriot Antiquities; the Charles Politis Collection of Ancient Greek Art. The Stathatos Mansion houses the Collection of Ancient Greek Art of the Academy of Athens, watercolours by James Skene, reproductions of ancient furniture and copies of drawings by the architect Ernst Ziller.

MUSEUM OF CYCLADIC ART
4 NEOPHYTOU DOUKA ST - ATHENS
TEL.: 2107228321-3

THE BYZANTINE AND CHRISTIAN MUSEUM

Founded in 1914, the Byzantine and Christian Museum was housed initially in the building of the Academy of Athens. In 1930 it was transferred permanently to the 'Ilissia' winter palace of the Duchess of Plaisance, in Vasilissis Sophias Avenue, a building constructed between 1840 and 1848 to plans by the architect Stamatis Kleanthis.

The Byzantine and Christian Museum is one of the most important in the world for its collections of Byzantine and Post-Byzantine art. It houses some 15,000 objects, treasures dating from the

Early Christian period to Post-Byzantine times (4th - 19th century), among them wood-carvings and wall-paintings, a large number of Byzantine portable icons, several thousand ecclesiastical works in the minor arts, elaborate crosses, patens, chalices, gold coins of the Byzantine empire, prelatic vestments, liturgical veils-*epitaphioi*, manuscripts, mosaics, copper-plate engravings, lithographs.

BYZANTINE AND CHRISTIAN MUSEUM
22 VASILISSIS SOPHIAS AVENUE
ATHENS
TEL.: 2107211027

THE WAR MUSEUM

Adjacent to the Byzantine and Christian Museum is an impressively large modern building, the War Museum of Greece, which opened in 1975. Displayed in its grounds are military aircraft and cannon from various periods. In the entrance hang portraits of the protagonists in the Greek War of Independence of 1821. The museum houses a diversity of weapons dating from the sixteenth to the twentieth century, from Greece and elsewhere. Ancient helmets, swords and shields, recent and contemporary armaments, military uniforms, banners, flags, military maps trace the development of martial history. The museum also has a good library with rich photographic material documenting the history of the Greek armed forces.

WAR MUSEUM
VASILISSIS SOPHIAS
AVENUE & 2 RIZARI ST
ATHENS
TEL.: 2107252974
TUESDAY-SATURDAY:
9.00-14.00 HRS
SUNDAY:
9.30-14.00 HRS
MONDAY: CLOSED

THE NATIONAL GALLERY

Although the National Gallery was founded officially in 1900, its nucleus existed already from the early years of the Greek State, when Ioannis Capodistrias was Governor. In 1878, it numbered 117 works and one year later a further 107 paintings were added, thanks to the donation of the lawyer and connoisseur Alexandros Soutsos, who expended his entire fortune on creating a museum of painting.

In 1954 the National Gallery was united with the Alexandros Soutsos Museum and in 1976 the building which houses the collections today was inaugurated.

The permanent collction of the National Gallery comprises paintings, sculptures and prints. Among its treasures are works by Domenicus Theotokopoulos (El Greco, 1541-1641), artists of the Ionian Islands School, nineteenth- and twentieth-century Greek painters. Among the most important nineteenth-century painters are Theodoros Vryzakis, who was inspired by the Greek Revolution of 1821, Nikephoros Lytras, Constantinos Volanakis, Nikolaos Gyzis, Georgios Iakovidis. The twentieth century is represented by: Constantinos Parthenis, Constantinos Maleas, Giannis Moralis, Giorgos Bouzianis, Nikos Hadjikyriakos-Ghikas, Giannis Tsarouchis, Nikos Engonopoulos, Dimitris Mytaras, Alexandros Fasianos, and others.

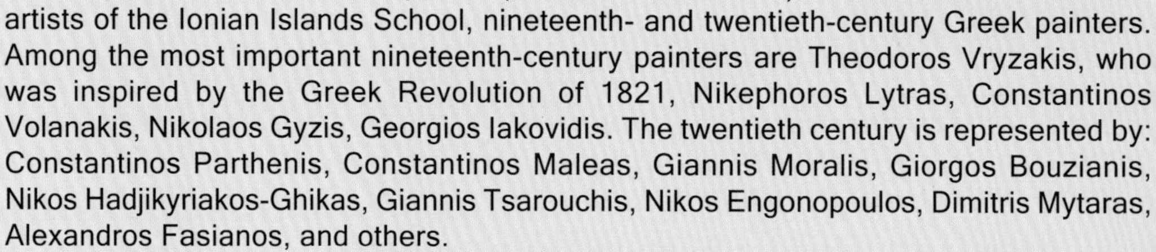

Throughout the year, temporary exhibitions are held in the National Gallery.

NATIONAL GALLERY
1 MICHALAKOPOULOU & 50 VASILEOS CONSTANTINOU ST - ATHENS TEL.: 2107235857
MONDAY, WEDNESDAY: 9.00-15.00 & 18.00-21.00 HRS
THURSDAY - SATURDAY: 9.00-15.00 HRS, SUNDAY: 10.00-14.00 HRS
TUESDAY: CLOSED

1

2

3

4

1. 'Waiting', 2.'The Carols': N. Lytras
3. 'The Betrothal', 4.'Memorizing': N. Gyzis
5. 'Theatre': N. Engonopoulos
6. 'The Concert of Angels': El. Greco

6

5

KOLONAKI SQUARE

Kolonaki Square takes its name from a remnant of times past, a small column (Gr. *kolonaki*) that stood at its centre. It is known also as Philike Hetaireia Square, which is why there is a bust of Emmanuel Xanthos, one of the founders of the Philike Hetaireia (Friendly Society), which was formed in the Russian city of Odessa, and prepared the way for the 1821 War of Independence.

The neighbourhood of Kolonaki developed around the square. Wealthy Athenian families built their residences here, so as to be at the hub of the high life focused on the monarchy and the palaces.

Several Neoclassical buildings still stand, most of them now housing embassies, museums, ministries and foreign haute-couture fashion houses. Luxury stores, cafes and restaurants complete the picture of Kolonaki

LYKABETTOS HILL

Lykabettos is the highest hill in Athens, rising about 280 metres a.s.l. It used to be totally barren but on the initiative of the Forestry Society it was planted with trees between 1890 and 1915. Lykabettos hill can be scaled easily by cable car, by automobile along the ring road, or on foot following the paths on its slopes. Perched on its summit is the nineteenth-century chapel of St George, while on its slopes is the Lykabettos Theatre, in which many concerts and theatrical performances are held in the summer. The view from the top of the hill is spectacular, reaching as far as the islands in the Saronic Gulf.

At the foot of Lykabettos is the Dexameni neighbourhood, so named after the reservoir (Gr. *dexameni*), construction of which commenced in the reign of Hadrian in AD 125 and was completed in the reign of Antoninus Pius in AD 140, in order to supply water to the city of Athens.

ΙΣΤΟΡΙΑ
ΑΡΧΑΙΟΛΟΓΙΑ
ΦΙΛΟΣΟΦΙΑ
ΟΘΩΝ Α.

THE UNIVERSITY AREA

The main thoroughfare of Athens, popularly known as Panepistimiou (i.e. University) street and officially as Eleftheriou Venizelou avenue, which starts at Syntagma Square and ends at Omonoia Square, runs through this area. This street is lined by interesting buildings associated with the administrative, economic and cultural life of the city, such as the Arsakeion (central law-courts), the National Library, the University, the Academy, the Eye Hospital, the Roman Catholic cathedral of St Denise, the Bank of Greece and the building of the Army Share Fund.

THE UNIVERSITY

On 2 July 1839, King Othon laid the foundation stone of the first of the three gems of Neoclassical architecture in Athens, the University. The building was designed by Christian Hansen and construction was completed in 1860. The University and two other buildings that flank it, the National Library and the Academy of Athens, comprise the 'trilogy' of Neoclassical Athens. The University building is simple yet majestic. Of rectangular plan, its façade consists of a portico with rectangular pillars and an Ionic propylon with central pediment. The interior of the portico is decorated with a mural by Karl Rahl, symbolizing the renaissance of Arts and Sciences in Greece. In front of the University are portrait statues of the national martyrs Rigas Feraios and Patriarch Gregory V, the man of letters Adamantios Korais and the first governor of independent Greece Ioannis Capodistrias.

THE ACADEMY

The Academy, the second of the trilogy of Neoclassical buildings, stands at the junction of Panepistimiou and Sina streets. Construction commenced in 1859, to plans by Theophilus Hansen, younger brother of the architect of the University, and financed by Baron Simon Sinas, a prominent figure in the economic life of Austria and Ambassor of Greece in Vienna. The building is almost entirely of Pentelic marble. The central part is in the form of an amphiprostyle Ionic temple, with elements inspired by the Erechtheion. The tympanum of the pediment carries a representation inspired by a pediment of the Parthenon, work of the sculptor Leonidas Drosis.

In front of the entrance to the Academy, set on two tall Ionic columns are statues of Apollo and Athena, and the seated portrait statues of Plato and Socrates, all works by the sculptor Leonidas Drosis.

THE NATIONAL LIBRARY

The third and last building of the so-called trilogy is located at the corner of Panepistimiou and Ippokratous streets. This too was designed by Theophilus Hansen and construction lasted from 1887 to 1902. It was financed by the Vagliano brothers, expatriate Greeks living in Russia.

Built of Pentelic marble, it has a propylon in the Doric order, to which lead two semicircular staircases of Renaissance style. In front of and inside the entrance stand portrait statues of the Vagliano brothers.

The National Library houses over 3,000,000 books, maps, prints, collections of newspapers, manuscript codices in Greek and in other languages, spanning the ninth to the twentieth century.

THE NUMISMATIC MUSEUM

The most representative example of the work of the German architect Ernst Ziller is the '*Iliou Melathron*' (= 'Palace of Troy'), residence of the German archaeologist Heinrich Schliemann. This mansion was commissioned by Schliemann, who named it the Iliou Melathron, and was decorated in a most luxurious manner. On the ceilings are representations from wall-paintings discovered at Pompeii, while the mosaic floors have motifs from finds discovered by Schliemann in his excavations at Troy and Mycenae. In 1927 the mansion was purchased by the Greek State and was for many years the seat of the Supreme Court.

Today it houses the Numismatic Museum of Athens. This is a modern museum in which are exhibited coins from ancient to recent times. Presented is the history of coins in relation to their place of provenance and the representations they carry on their flan. Among the rare and unique coins in the museum are an issue of a silver Attic didrachm of 460 BC, with head of Athena and an owl with open wings, and a signed coin of Syracuse with representation of a chariot with Nike, work of the engraver Kimon.

NUMISMATIC MUSEUM
21 PANEPISTIMIOU ST
TEL.: 2103643774
TUESDAY - SUNDAY:
8.00-14.30 HRS
MONDAY: CLOSED

THE NATIONAL HISTORICAL MUSEUM

The National Historical Museum is housed in one of the most important buildings of Athens, the Old Parliament in Stadiou street. Until 1834, when it was bought by the Greek State, this was the home of A. Kontostavlos, one of the wealthiest merchants in the city. Between 1834 and 1836 it served as the residence of King Othon. From 1843 until 1854, when it was destroyed by fire, it was the seat of the Greek Parliament.

Construction of the new building began in 1858, to plans by the French architect François-Louis-Florimond Boulanger, and was completed in 1871, after modifications to the design by the Greek architect Panagiotis Kalkos, From 1875 until 1931 it was once again the seat of the Greek Parliament. From 1931 until 1961 this building housed the Ministry of Justice and from 1962 onwards the National Historical Museum.

Exhibited in its rooms are heirlooms dating from the time of the Fall of Constantinople to the Second World War, prints by nineteenth-century travellers, and watercolours. On display are portraits of philhellenes, freedom-fighters, members of the Philike Hetaireia, flags, weapons, costumes-uniforms of protagonists in the Greek War of Independence. Notable too are the personal effects of freedom-fighters, politicians and others, such as the helmet and weapons of Theodoros Kolokotronis, the musket of Athanasios Diakos, the lute of Makrygiannis, items belonging to Lord Byron.

Outside the building, front and back, are portrait statues of Charilaos Trikoupis, work of Thomas Thomopoulos, and Theodoros Deligiannis, work of Georgios Dimitriadis. In the small square in front of the building is the equestrian statue of Theodoros Kolokotronis, work of Lazaros Sochos.

NATIONAL HISTORICAL MUSEUM
13 STADIOU ST
TEL.: 2103237617
TUESDAY - SUNDAY: 9.00-14.00 HRS
MONDAY: CLOSED

KLAFTHMONOS SQUARE

This is one of the oldest and most central squares in the historical heart of Athens, which has changed name several times.

It was known initially as 25 March Square. During the reign of King Othon it was renamed Aeschylus Square and when the Mint opened there it was called Nomismatokopeion (Mint) Square.

Later, after Othon was deposed, it became Eleftheria (Freedom) Square, and when the Mint became the Ministry of Finance, in the reign of King George I, it took the name Klafthmonos Square. This last name is due to the fact that after each change in government civil servants were fired, and they gathered in the square in front of the ministry to weep (Gr. *kleo*), in order to be reinstated. In 1989 the square was renamed once more, as National Reconciliation (Ethniki Symphiliosi) Square.

THE MUSEUM OF THE CITY OF ATHENS

The Museum of the City of Athens was founded in 1973 and began operating in 1980. It is housed in a Neoclassical mansion in Paparrigopoulou street, adjacent to Klafthmonos Square. The building is known also as the 'Old Palace' because the first monarchs of Modern Greece, King Othon and Queen Amalia, lived here for about seven years.

The museum is dedicated to the recent history of Athens and exhibited in it is the art collection of its founder, Lambros Eftaxias, which includes paintings, furniture, prints, domestic vessels and historical heirlooms from the Frankish period to the nineteenth century. Also displayed are authentic pieces of furniture belonging to Othon and Amalia, watercolours, prints and paintings by foreign travellers who visited Athens. Particularly spectacular is the scale model of Athens in 1842, made by the architect Ioannis Travlos.

MUSEUM OF THE CITY OF ATHENS
7 PAPARRIGOPOULOU ST
TEL.: 2103246164
MONDAY, WEDNESDAY, THURSDAY, FRIDAY: 09.00-16.00 HRS
SATURDAY & SUNDAY: 10.00-15.00 HRS

THE CHURCH OF SAINTS THEODORE

On the southwest side of Klafthmonos Square stands the eleventh-century Byzantine church of Sts Theodore. Incorporated in the wall above its west entrance is an inscription recording its founding. The church was damaged during the 1821 Greek War of Independence and was repaired in 1840. It is of cross-in-square plan with a dome of Athenian type, which means that it follows the cruciform shape and is not horizontal. The cloisonné masonry is variegated by interesting decorative brickwork.

THE ROMAN CATHOLIC CATHEDRAL

The Roman Catholic cathedral is situated at the corner of Eleftheriou Venizelou (Panepistimiou) and Omirou streets, and is dedicated to St Denise (St Dionysios). The original plans were by Leo von Klenze but these were modified by Lysandros Kaftantzoglou. Construction began in 1853 and was completed in 1865.

The church is a three-aisled basilica with an imposing marble staircase at the entrance and a bell tower, which is slightly higher than its roof.

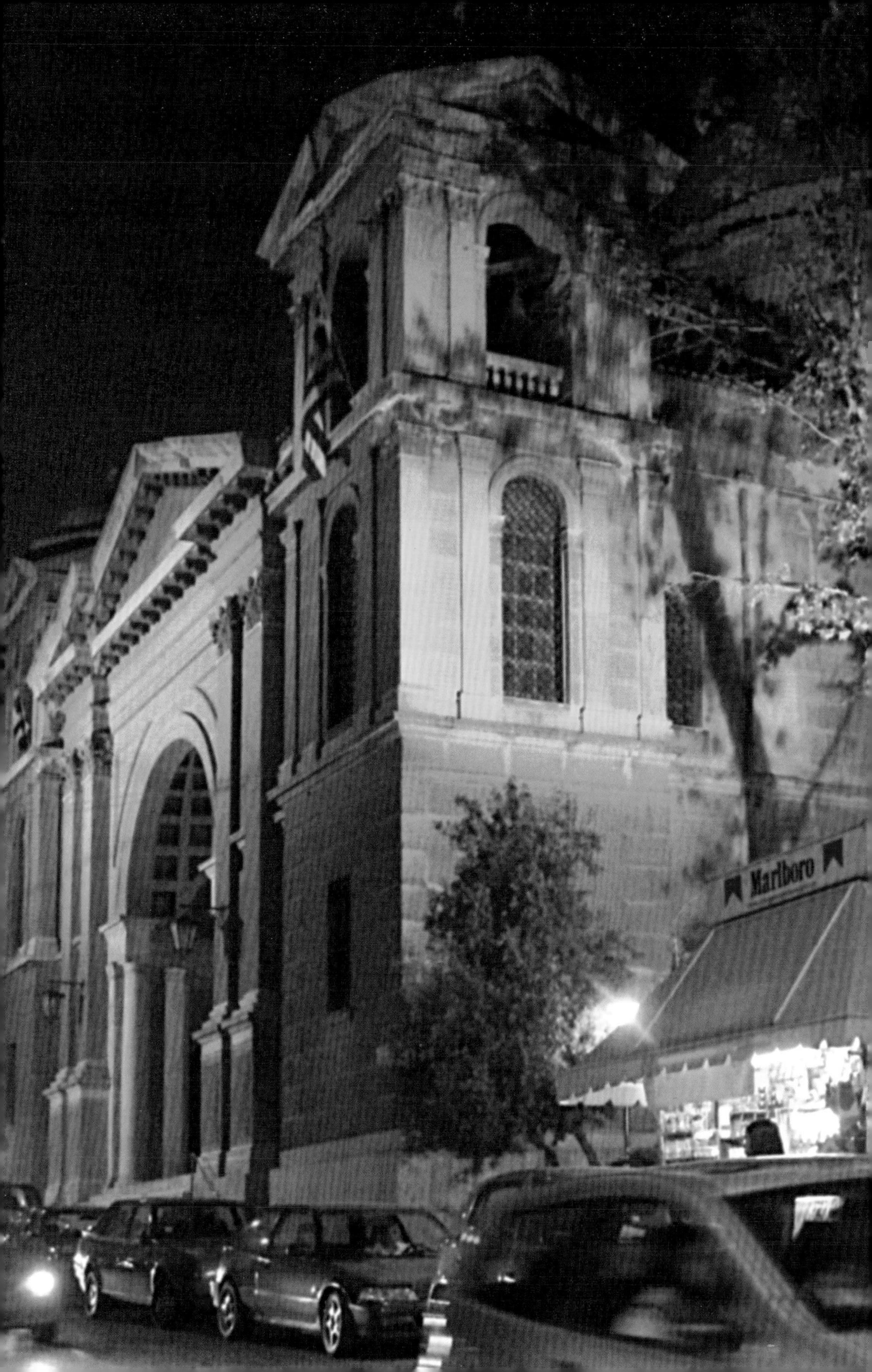
Marlboro

THE AREA OF OMONOIA SQUARE

In the area of Omonoia Square and the streets around it, the sophisticated cosmopolitan and the popular working-class centre of the city meet. The City Hall (Demarcheion), the Central Market, the shops selling traditional wares, the high-rise department stores and the large hotels in this part of the city are characteristic elements of its administrative, economic, cultural and commercial life.

OMONOIA SQUARE

The square's history begins with the first plans drafted for the capital of the Greek State. According to the urban plan of Kleanthis and Schaubert, this was where the palace would be built, along with the most important buildings in the city. However, this plan was never implemented and only the square remained, at that time named Othon Square. In 1862, after King Othon was deposed, it was renamed Omonia (Concord) Square. A nodal point in the city, it is a transit centre for Greeks, Athenians, immigrants, tourists, entrepreneurs and journeymen.

The square is circular and from it radiate the main streets of Athens Panepistimiou, Stadiou, Athinas, Agiou Constantinou, 3 Septemvriou. It has witnessed major historic moments and hosted political rallies, protests, street barricades, victory celebrations of sports fans, and so on.

Over the years, its aspect has changed many times, but some buildings survive as mementoes of its past, among them the Alexander the Great Hotel and the Bangeion Hotel, at the junction with Athinas street, and the building with the historical Neon coffee shop in its ground floor, on the side towards 3 Septemvriou street.

CITY HALL (DEMARCHEION) SQUARE

City Hall (Demarcheion) Square, popularly known as Kotzias Square and officially named National Resistance (Ethniki Antistasi) Square, is located to the south of Omonoia Square, on Athinas street. It was called originally Ludwig Square, in honour of the king of Bavaria and father of Othon, but after Othon had been deposed it was renamed New Theatre Square. In 1888, the Civic Theatre of Athens, designed by Ernst Ziller, was built at its centre. Although many famous Greek and foreign actors trod the boards of its stage, the theatre was, alas, demolished in 1939. The demolition order was signed by the government minister C. Kotzias, whose name, by tragic irony, was subsequently given to the square.

On the west side of the square stands the City Hall (Demarcheion) of Athens, a two-storey Neoclassical building erected between 1872 and 1874, to plans by the architect Panagiotis Kalkos.

The mural decorations in its interior are by Photis Kontoglou and Giorgos Gounaropoulos, and depict scenes from

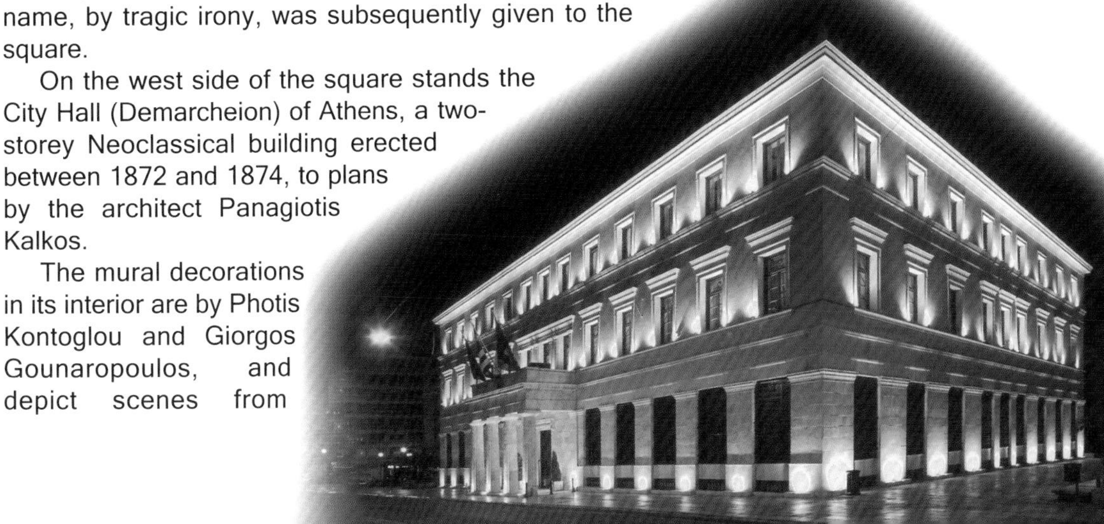

Greek history and mythology. On the east side of the square is the headquarters of the National Bank of Greece. This Neoclassical building was originally two separate buildings, the England Hotel and the Dounados mansion, which were joined together in 1895 and have housed the National Bank since 1901. On the south side of the square is the Melas mansion, designed by Ernst Ziller and inaugurated in 1874. From 1900 until 1972 it was the headquarters of the Hellenic Postal Services. In the course of earth-removal works to construct an underground car park in City Hall Square, ancient pottery workshops and part of an ancient cemetery were discovered and excavated.

THE PSYRRI NEIGHBOURHOOD

Psyrri is one of the oldest working-class neighbourhoods of Athens, located between Monastiraki, Metaxourgeion and Kerameikos. Until a few years ago, Psyrri was a mosaic of humble houses, numerous churches, small manufacturing businesses, machine shops and workshops.

Today this picture has changed radically. The neighbourhood is being upgraded continuously and has developed into the *par excellence* place where young people hang out. Bars, clubs, restaurants, theatres and *mezes* bars with live music create a lively entertainment scene, especially at night, when the streets are much busier than during the day.

ΠΛΑΤΕΙΑ ΗΡΩΩΝ
ΠΛΑΤΕΙ
ΗΡΩΩΝ
IROON
1924

THE NATIONAL THEATRE

The National Theatre is located in Agiou Constantinou street. The foundation stone was laid in 1895 and the building was inaugurated in 1901. Built to plans by Ernst Ziller, the theatre has features of theatres in European cities, such as Vienna and Copenhagen. A magnificent building in the Italian Renaissance style, it was named originally the Royal Theatre of Athens and was the privileged venue of 'the few' until 1908. Later, after the abolition of the monarchy in Greece, it was renamed the National Theatre and opened its doors to the city's public. Three of the five stages under its aegis are now housed in the Neoclassical building designed by Ziller.

THE CHURCH OF SAINT CONSTANTINE

In 1869 the city council decided to build a church dedicated to St Constantine, to honour the birth of the Crown Prince, later King Constantine I. The large and imposing church in the Greek style was constructed to plans by architect Lysandros Kaftantzoglou and was consecrated in 1893.

THE POLYTECHNEION

On the plot of land between Patission, Tositsa, Bouboulinas and Stournara streets stands a complex of Neoclassical buildings erected with donations from Michael Tositsas, Nikolaos Stournaris, Georgios Averoff, and to plans by Lysandros Kaftantzoglou.

The complex consists of three basic buildings. The central one is two-storeyed with marble staircases leading to a propylon with four Ionic columns. In front of this, to left and to right, are two other one-storey buildings with propylon with Doric columns.

In November 1973 the Polytechneion (National Technical University of Athens) was the focus of the student uprising against the military dictatorship that had seized power in 1967. On the night of the 17 November, while the building was thronged with students and ordinary people, the junta ordered a tank to break through the main gate, mowing down everyone and everything in its path, and, together with the army and the police, quashing the rebellion. Despite the high toll of dead and injured, this event hastened the fall of the dictatorship.

Since then the Polytechneion is a historic monument and in its forecourt is a sculpture of a gigantic head fallen on the ground, work of Memos Makris, to commemorate the young people who lost their life on that terrible night of 1973.

THE NATIONAL ARCHAEOLOGICAL MUSEUM

The 'Harpist' from Keros

The National Archaeological Museum is situated just beyond the Polytechneion in Patission street. Founded in the late nineteenth century, it is the largest and most important museum in Greece for the study of ancient Greek civilization.

The earliest exhibits date from the Neolithic Age, that is, from the end of the seventh millennium to around 3000 BC, and come mainly from the citadels at Sesklo and Dimini, sites near Volos in Thessaly, as well as from elsewhere in Greece and from Troy. Steatopygous female figurines with emphasized breasts and buttocks, a figurine of a female holding a baby in her arms (*kourotrophos*), a statuette of a

seated male with pronounced genitalia, numerous stone and bone tools for everyday use, and clay vases monochrome, with painted decoration or undecorated are some of the Neolithic objects on display.

The next unit in the museum is dedicated to the Early Cycladic Culture, which developed in the Cyclades between the early third and the end of the second millennium BC. It is a singular culture with its own distinctive character. The figurines and the vases of white marble, of simple yet very elegant forms, bring to mind modern sculptures. Outstanding in this collection are two male figurines of musicians: one standing and playing a double 'flute' (*aulos*), and the other sitting on a lovely throne and playing a kind of harp. Of interest among the clay vessels are the so-called 'frying-pan vases', which are hollow on one side and flat with incised decoration on the other.

Cycladic figurine

The Mycenaean Collection, representative of the Mycenaean Civilization (1580-1100 BC), is the most splendid in the museum. The gold funerary masks that covered the face of the dead, the exquisite jewellery, the rings with diverse intricate representations on the bezel, the bronze daggers with gold and silver decoration, the superb repoussé gold cups from Vapheio, the 'Warrior Krater', the ivory miniatures, the lovely bull's-head rhyton with gold horns, and the wonderful wall-paintings from Tiryns and Mycenae, vindicate Homer, who gave to Mycenae the epithet '*polychryses*', meaning 'rich in gold'.

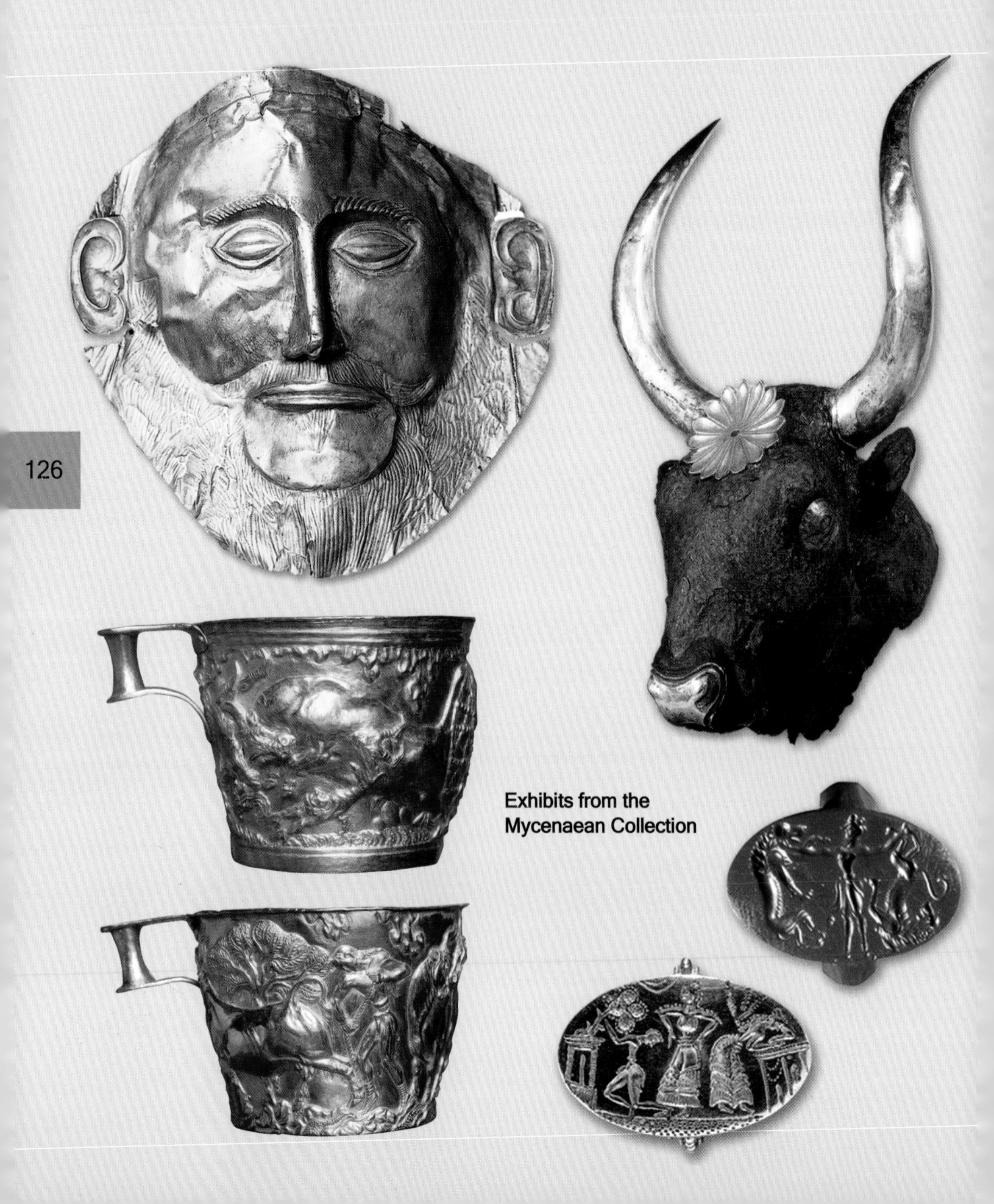

Exhibits from the Mycenaean Collection

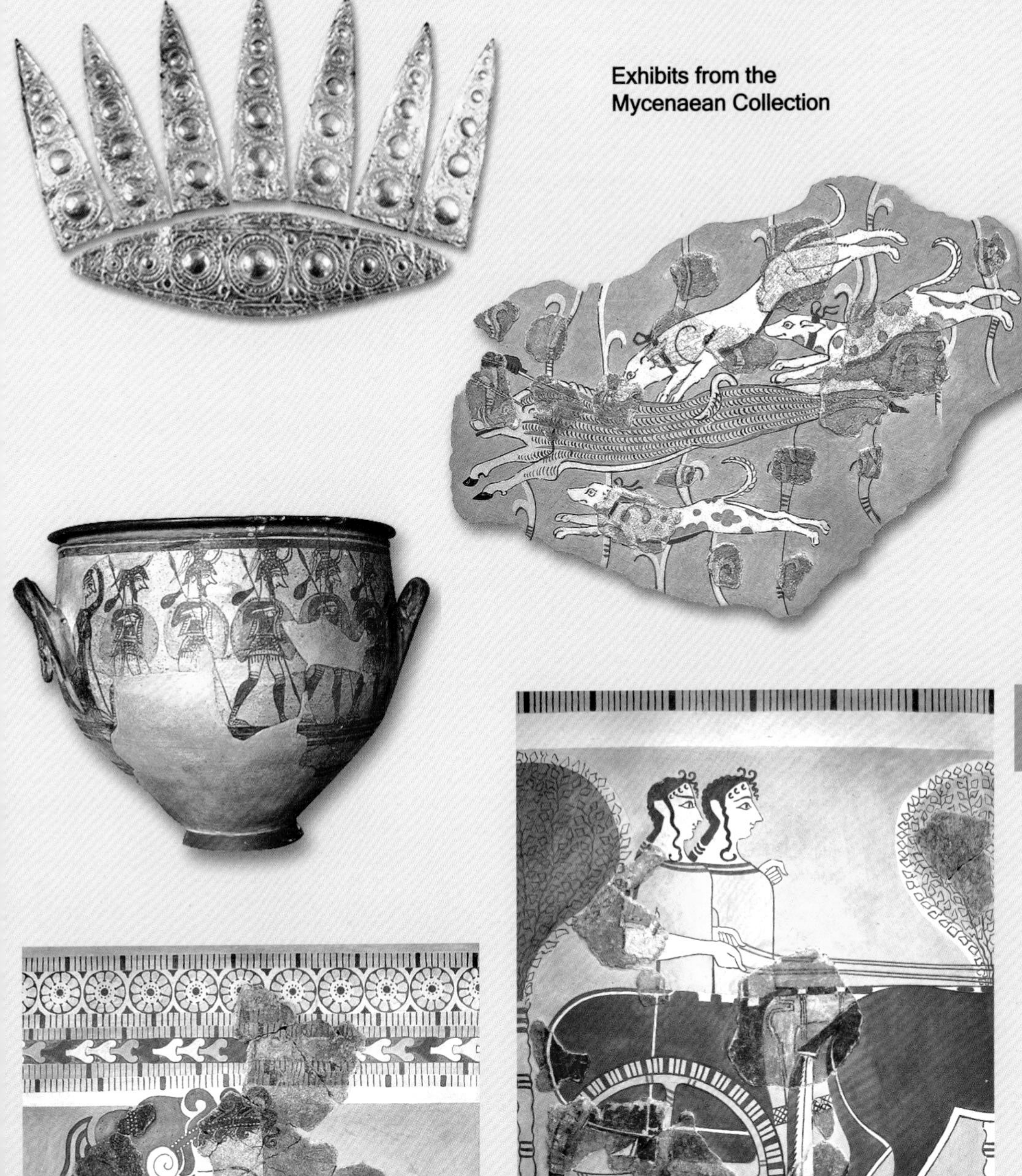

Exhibits from the
Mycenaean Collection

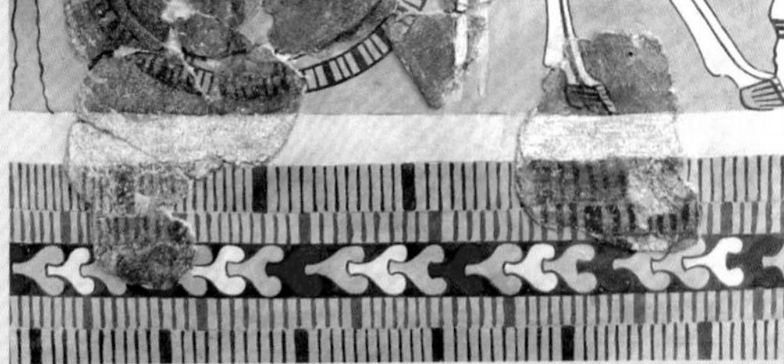

The following chronological period, the Geometric, was named thus after the large clay vases with geometric decoration. A representative example is the large clay amphora, approximately 1.60 metres high, found at the Dipylon. It is dated to around 750 BC and is decorated with many variations of meander pattern and, in the middle, the figure of the deceased surrounded by lamenting mourners.

Around 700 BC Archaic sculpture appeared, creating a tradition that lasted two hundred years. The most characteristic creations of the Archaic period are the *kouroi* and the *korai*. Either funerary statues set up on graves or votive offerings dedicated in sanctuaries, these figures were represented at first in strictly frontal pose with the arms stuck to the sides of the body. Gradually, the articulation of the human body began to be modelled more naturally. So, the statues became more lifelike, with the left leg to the fore, the arms bent at the elbow and a smile on the face. The collection of sculptures and statues from the Classical period

Grave stele of a javelin-thrower

The Dipylon amphora

that followed includes such impressive exhibits as the bronze statues of Zeus or Poseidon from Artemision (450 BC), the Ephebe of Antikythera and the comely Marathon Boy. Outstanding among the reliefs of the period is a large marble work with representation of Demeter, goddess of agriculture, handing a sheaf of wheat to Triptolemos, while behind him her daughter Persephone watches the scene. Many marble funerary monuments date from the Classical period, such as the grave stele of Hegeso and the lekythos of Myrrhine.

The Anavyssos Kouros

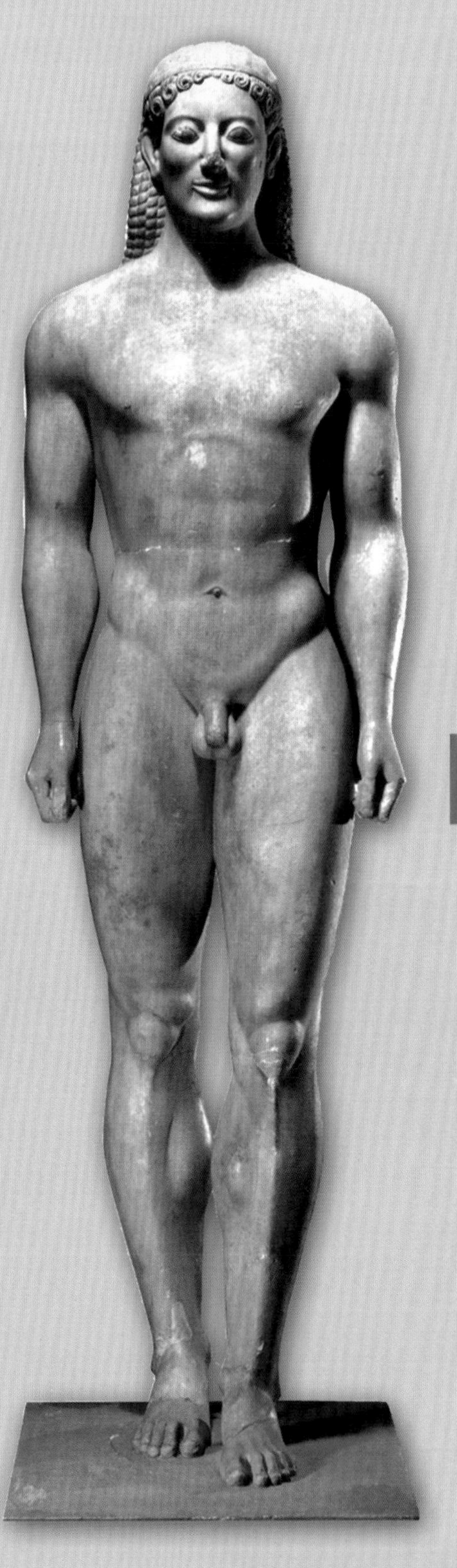

'The Fisherman', wall-painting from Thera

One other important exhibit is the Varvakeion Athena, a small copy in marble of Pheidias' chryselephantine statue in the Parthenon. The 'Diadoumenos', statue of a youth crowning himself with a fillet, is a Roman copy of the masterpiece by the sculptor Polykleitos. The little jockey with expressive face, recovered from the sea off Cape Artemision, is another of the museum's *chefs d' oeuvre*. The museum also houses other very interesting collections, such as the collection of small works in bronze, of jewellery donated by Helen Stathatos, the Egyptian Collection and the Thera Collection with the impressive Late Bronze Age wall-paintings from Akrotiri.

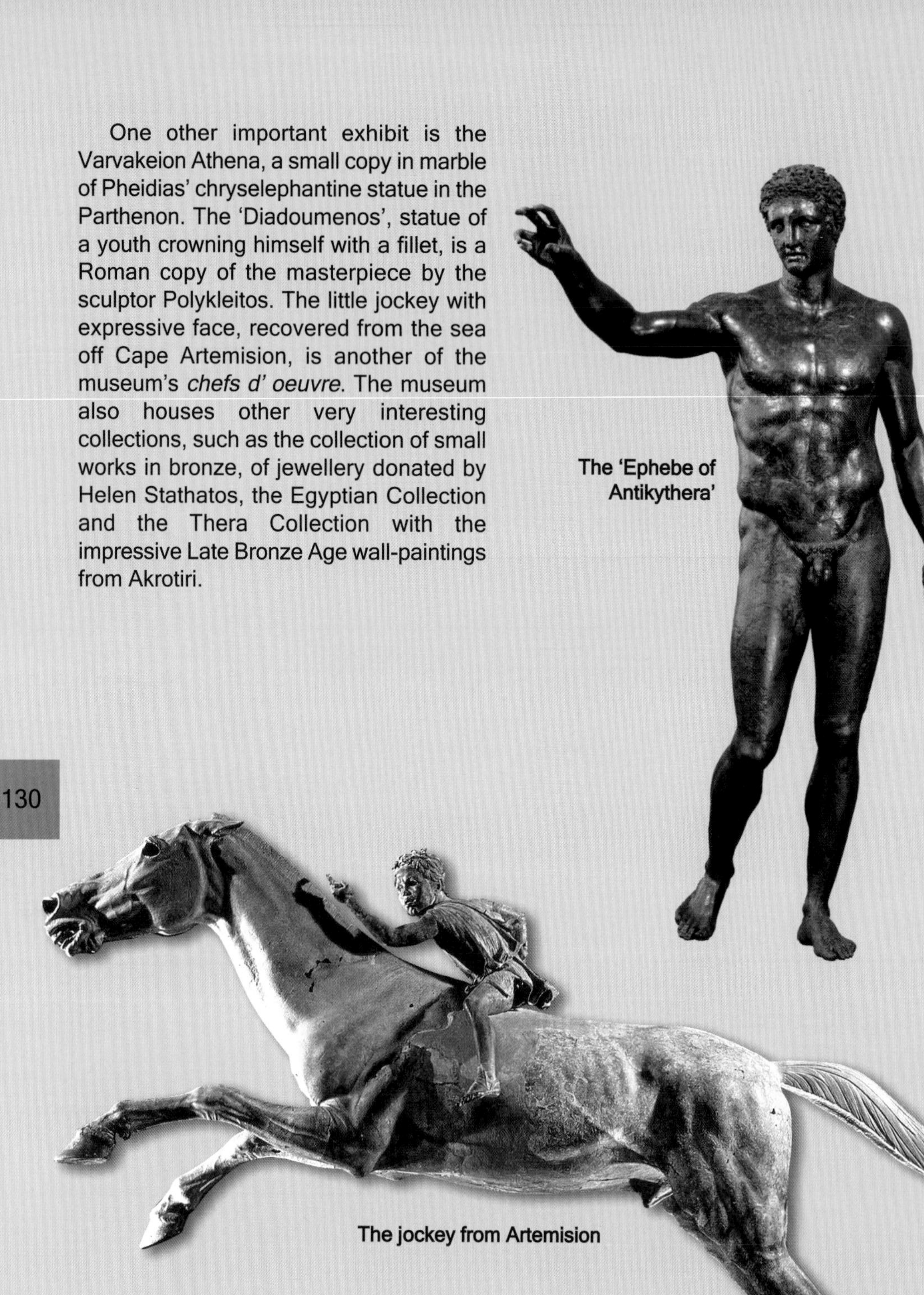

The 'Ephebe of Antikythera'

The jockey from Artemision

NATIONAL ARCHAEOLOGICAL MUSEUM
44 PATISSION ST
TEL.: 2108217717
TUESDAY - SUNDAY: 8.30-15.00 HRS
MONDAY: CLOSED

THE EPIGRAPHICAL MUSEUM

On the south side of the National Archaeological Museum is the Epigraphical Museum, which is entered from Tositsa street. Housed in its eleven rooms is the largest collection of inscriptions (over 13,000) in the world, spanning the seventh century BC to the fourth century AD. The overwhelming majority is in Greek. Among the exhibits of great historical importance are lists of cities, *demoi*, tribes, priests, athletes victorious in games, and decrees voted by cities. There are also inscriptions of religious content, inscriptions relating to the development of the Greek language, and pedestals of statues with the signatures of their sculptors.

EPIGRAPHICAL MUSEUM
1 TOSITSA ST
TEL.: 2108217637
TUESDAY - SUNDAY: 8.30-15.00 HRS
MONDAY: CLOSED

IN THE VICINITY OF ATHENS

THE KAISARIANI MONASTERY

The Kaisariani monastery, which dates from the eleventh century, stands amidst pine and cypress trees on a picturesque slope of Mount Hymettos.

Ancient marbles (*spolia*) from the sanctuaries of the deities worshipped hereabouts (Aphrodite, Demeter) in Antiquity have left their traces in the masonry of the katholikon, the lintel of the refectory and even the fountain, in which an ancient marble ram's head, which comes from an Archaic building of the Acropolis, has been placed. In Antiquity, there were many burbling springs of crystal-clear water, which was believed to have miraculous powers, increasing fertility, protecting pregnancy and curing barrenness in women.

The monastery was named either after the monk who founded it, who was perhaps called Caesarius (Kaisarios), or after an epithet of the Virgin, 'Syriani', or after an icon of the Virgin, which came from Caesarea (Kaisareia). Located inside the precinct of the monastery complex are a bathhouse, which follows the tradition of the Roman *thermae*, the monks' cells, the refectory and the kitchen with chimneystack, as well as the katholikon, which is dedicated to the Presentation of the Virgin in the Temple (*Eisodia tes Theotokou*). The narthex of the katholikon, the side-chapel (*parekklesion*) of St Anthony, the bell-tower and the rest of the buildings of the monastery were constructed later, during the Ottoman period. At that time, as well as earlier in the Byzantine Age, the monastery was an important spiritual centre, with a very rich library and a school.

The katholikon is of cruciform plan with a dome that rests on four columns with Ionic capitals. It is of strictly geometrical construction in cloisonné masonry without dentil bands, relieved by decorative brickwork restricted to parallel curves above the windows. Noteworthy is the marble templon-screen, made of materials from an Early Christian church.

The wall-paintings, distinguished by the harmonious colours, the balanced arrangement of the compositions and the serene expression of the figures, are of so-called Cretan art and are dated to the sixteenth century. The wall-paintings in the narthex were executed in the seventeenth century by the Peloponnesian artist Ioannis Hypatos.

KAISARIANI MONASTERY
TEL.: 2107236619
TUESDAY - SUNDAY:
08.30-15.00 HRS
MONDAY: CLOSED

THE DAPHNI MONASTERY

Christ Pantocrator

The Daphni monastery, the largest, the most splendid and the most important Byzantine monument of Athens, is located at the 9th kilometre on the national highway linking Athens and Corinth.

It was built in the sixth century AD on the site of an ancient sanctuary of Apollo Daphnephoros, many architectural members (*spolia*) from which were reused in its construction. Indeed, it seems that it owes its name to Apollo Daphnephoros, even though there are other explanations, such as that of the queen Daphne whose endangered ship escaped wreck and who thanked God for her salvation by building the monastery and gifting to it her entire fortune of countless gold florins in barrels.

After a period of decline, the monastery was reorganized in the eleventh century and the present katholikon was built. This is a church of octagon plan, built of poros ashlar blocks and bricks, according to the cloisonné system. The large dome is 8 metres in diameter and 5.27 metres high from its base, The interior is divided into the sanctuary, the nave, the narthex and the porch, the Gothic arches of which are a later addition made in the period of Frankish rule. The Daphni monastery is famed for its exquisite mosaics, executed with tesserae of white marble from Pentele, yellowish marble from Paros, blue from Hymettos and black from Eleusis, upon a glistening gold ground. They date from the late eleventh century. Depicted on the large surfaces are scenes from the Life of the Virgin and from the Life of Christ, while on the smaller surfaces are figures of prophets, saints and martyrs, as well as scenes from the Scriptures. In addition to the predominant gold, white too is prominent, in the saints' chitons, the angels' wings and the Virgin's robe. Elements of the paintings, such as Christ's body in the Baptism, which is not concealed by the waves but is clearly visible and anatomically correct, the dignified and slightly melancholic figures of some youthful saints and angels, which are reminiscent of ancient ephebes, the saints who closely resemble ancient philosophers rather than sun-burnt ascetics of the desert, reveal that the mosaicist was influenced by the ancient Classical spirit. Dominating the dome is Christ Pantocrator, with his wrinkled forehead and his stern, piercing gaze.

The heyday of the monastery was short-lived. In the thirteenth century the Franks came and used it as a burial ground. Shortly after, monks of the Cistercian order were installed here, followed by the Ottomans, and in the sixteenth century Orthodox monks returned. The monastery was finally abandoned in the early nineteenth century.

PIRAEUS

Piraeus has been the harbour of Athens since ancient times and is today the largest port in Greece. It lies some 10 kilometres from the centre of Athens, on the northeast shore of the Saronic Gulf.

Principal feature of Piraeus is its three natural harbours: the Central Harbour or Kantharos, the Zea harbour or Pashalimani, and the Mikrolimano (= small harbour) or Mounichia harbour.

The history of Piraeus begins in the fifth century BC, when Themistocles proposed to the Athenians that they build a fleet and safe harbours. It was then decided to transfer the outport of Athens from Phaleron to the Piraeus. In 439 BC, the Athenians began building the fortifications of the new port, which were completed after the end of the Persian War, with the construction of the Long Walls linking Athens with the Piraeus. Thus, a single settlement was created, with Athens functioning as political and religious centre, and the Piraeus as commercial and military. In the decade 470-460 BC, the architect and urban planner Hippodamos from Miletos was commissioned to build the city of Piraeus. He applied the famous Hippodamian system, namely the division of space into a grid of uniform building plots intersected vertically by parallel streets.

After their defeat by the Spartans in the Peloponnesian War, the Athenians were forced to demolish the Long Walls, which were rebuilt in 394 BC by Konon. In 86 BC the Piraeus was put to the torch by the Roman general Sulla. It sunk into decline and never recovered until 1843. During these years Piraeus came to be known as Porto di Leone, because of a large marble lion that stood in its central harbour. This statue was taken to Venice by

Morosini and there is now a replica in its place.

From 1834 onwards, Piraeus developed rapidly and is now one of the biggest ports in the Mediterranean. It is a modern commercial centre with many monuments and remains from the previous centuries. The most notable is the city's fortification, which survives in several places. The wall constructed by Konon survives along the coast of the Peiraike peninsula and for a length of about two and a half kilometres

In Antiquity there were five commercial stoas in the central harbour, known as Kantharos the present Akti Miaouli. These were called the Deigma because there the merchants took samples (Gr. *deigmata*) of their merchandise. Visible on the west side of the harbour are remains of the Eetioneia Gate, one of the most important gates in the wall. Close by was a sanctuary dedicated to Aphrodite Euploia, patron goddess of seafaring. On the northwest side of the Zea harbour, which was for military use, the foundations of the Skeuotheke have been revealed. Designed by the architect Philon in around 330 BC, this building was intended for storing ships' tackle and equipment, such as anchors, sails, oars, ropes. The entrance to it is preserved in the free space of an apartment building in Ypsilantou street. The third harbour of the Piraeus, the Mounichia harbour, was also for military purposes. Next to the present premises of the Yacht Club are remains attesting to the existence of a sanctuary of Artemis Mounichia.

Piraeus still has quite a few Neoclassical buildings at different points in the city, amongst the modern constructions. One of these is the Municipal Theatre in Vasileos Georgiou street, a handsome and majestic building of 1895.

THE PIRAEUS ARCHAEOLOGICAL MUSEUM

Located between the commercial harbour and the Zea harbour, the museum was refurbished in 1998. One of the major archaeological museums in Greece, it houses finds of the Classical, Hellenistic and Roman periods, from the area of Piraeus as well as from the Mesogeia and the islands in the Saronic Gulf.

Among its most impressive

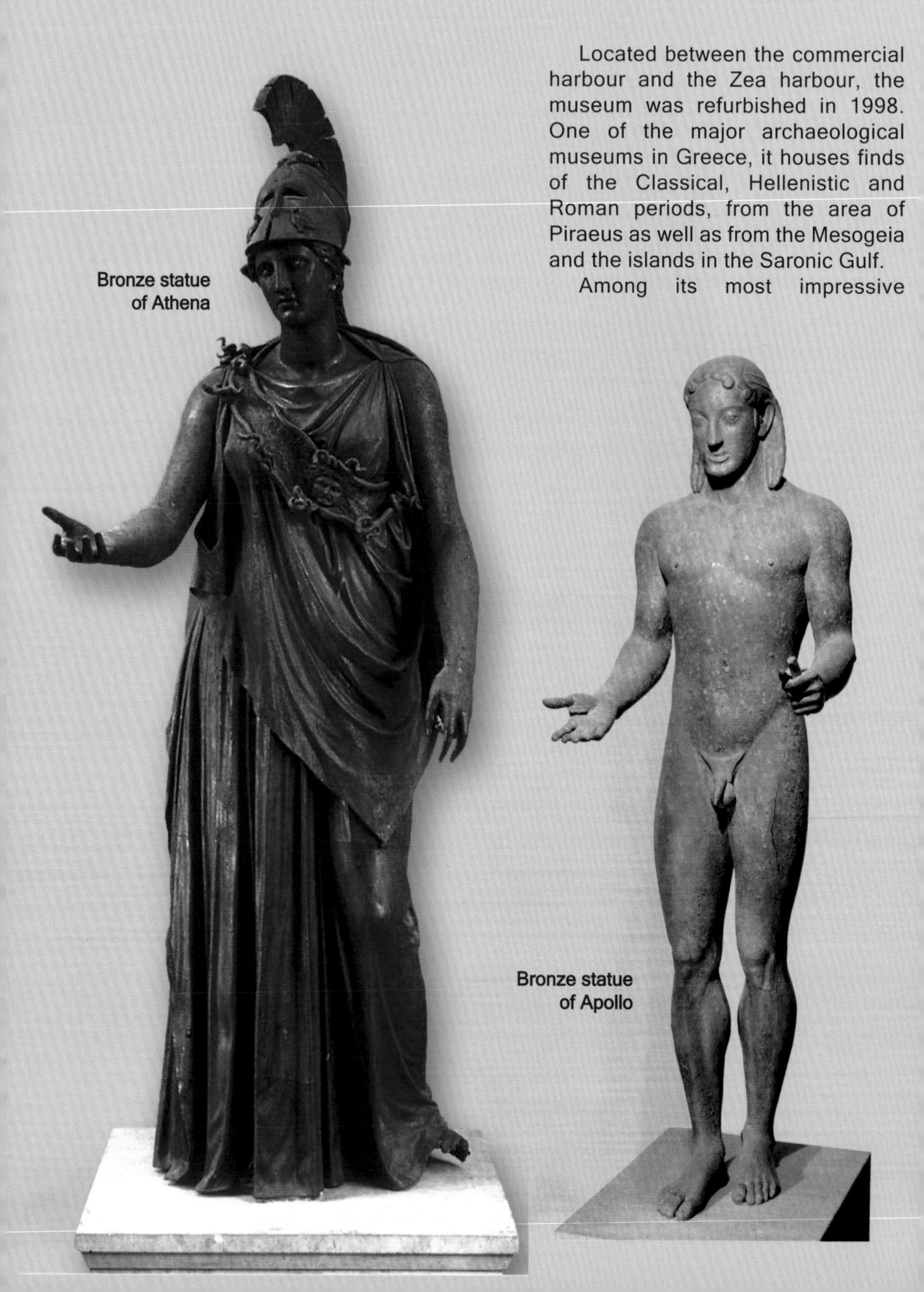

Bronze statue of Athena

Bronze statue of Apollo

exhibits are the four bronze statues one of Apollo of 500 BC, two of Artemis and one of Athena of the fourth century BC. The statue of Athena is 2.45 metres high and the goddess is represented wearing a Corinthian helmet embellished with griffins and owls. Also of great merit are the funerary monuments, outstanding among which is the seven-metre high temple-shaped monument of the fourth century BC, which was found in the district of Kallithea.

Bronze statue of Artemis

PIRAEUS ARCHAEOLOGICAL MUSEUM
31 CHARILAOU TRIKOUPI ST - PIRAEUS
TEL.: 2104521598
TUESDAY - SUNDAY: 9.00-15.00 HRS
MONDAY: CLOSED

THE MARITIME MUSEUM OF GREECE

This important museum houses about 2,000 exhibits associated with the maritime history of Greece. Particularly interesting is the collection of models of ships, both ancient and modern, such as the *Olympias* and the battleship *Psara*. Maps, weapons, flags, naval uniforms, busts of admirals and paintings depicting sea battles complete the museum's exhibits. Last, visitors can also see part of the Themistoclean Wall, which has been incorporated into the wall of the Maritime Museum.

MARITIME MUSEUM OF GREECE
AKTI THEMISTOKLEOUS - PIRAEUS
TEL.: 2104516264
TUESDAY - SATURDAY: 9.00-14.00 HRS
SUNDAY - MONDAY: CLOSED

ELEUSIS

Twenty-three kilometres west of Athens is the town of Eleusis, with one of the most important archaeological sites in Greece. In Antiquity Eleusis was a major cult centre of Demeter and Persephone.

According to myth, Demeter was goddess of agriculture and fertility, and mother of Persephone from her union with Zeus. One day, as Persephone was picking flowers with her girlfriends, the god Pluto abducted her and took her to his kingdom in the Underworld. For nine days and nine nights, Demeter wandered all over the world in search of her daughter, eventually reaching the palace of King Keleus at Eleusis. There she recounted her story, and as recompense for the hospitality she received, she taught Keleus' son, Triptolemos, the art of cultivating cereals. Demeter ceased to be interested in the fertility of the soil and in solitude mourned the loss of her daughter. Men began to starve. Nothing sprouted from the earth, not a seed germinated, until Zeus intervened and Demeter and Pluto agreed that Persephone would spend one third of the year in the company of her husband and the remaining months with her mother. Demeter, happy with this arrangement, allowed the earth to bear fruit again.

The principal rites associated with the worship of Demeter and Persephone were the Eleusinian Mysteries. Initially these were a local festival, but after the annexation of Eleusis to Athens by Solon in the sixth century BC, the Eleusinian Mysteries became an Athenian festival.

Eleusis was connected to Athens by the Sacred Way (*Hiera Hodos*), the road along which the procession of the Mysteries passed. During the tyranny of Peisistratos, in the sixth century BC, the Telesterion was constructed at Eleusis. This was the most important building in the sanctuary, centre of the cult of Demeter, and a wall was raised around this area. The sanctuary was destroyed by the Persians in 479 BC and was renovated later by Pericles. It enjoyed its final heyday in Roman times, when the emperors Hadrian, Antoninus Pius and Marcus Aurelius built many edifices, the Lesser and the Great Propylaia among them. In AD 379, when Theodosius issued the edict banning the worship of the ancient gods, the Mysteries and the sanctuary fell into decline. Eleusis was destroyed by the Visigoths under Alarich, in AD 395.

On entering the archaeological site, visitors see a Roman court paved with rectangular marble flags, and two triumphal arches, to the left and the right of it. In the middle of the court is the temple of Artemis Propylaia and Poseidon Patros. Behind the

arches were inns and bathhouses. To the south of the temple are the remains of the Great Propylaia, which copied the Propylaia of the Athenian Acropolis. To the left of them is the 'Kallichoron Phrear' or 'Well of the Fair Dances', where, myth has it, Demeter sat down to rest when she arrived at Eleusis. Behind the Great Propylaia were the Lesser Propylaia, the entrance to the main area of the sanctuary. This gateway was adorned with two figures of Karyatids, one of which is in the local archaeological museum and the other in Great Britain. To the right of the entrance are the foundations of a small building, which is said to have been the temple of Pluto and the entrance to the Underworld. Proceeding onwards, visitors come to the most sacred and most important building at Eleusis, the Telesterion. Of square plan, large dimensions and provided with six doorways two on its north, east and south sides, the Telesterion held 3,000 persons. At the centre was a rectangular building, the Anaktoron, in which the sacred attributes of Demeter were kept.

In the rest of the space of the sanctuary there were temples, cisterns, storerooms, a bouleuterion of the fourth century BC, a gymnasium of the Roman period and other buildings.

THE ELEUSIS ARCHAEOLOGICAL MUSEUM

The Eleusis Archaeological Museum was built in 1889 and is situated to the southwest of the Telesterion. It houses finds from the west cemetery of Eleusis and the sanctuary. Exhibited in the forecourt are column capitals from the Lesser Propylaia, sculptures and a marble sarcophagus of the second century AD.

The objects displayed in the interior of the museum are from various periods. Noteworthy are a large amphora decorated with a depiction of Odysseus Blinding Polyphemos(650 BC), a headless statue of Demeter by the sculptor Agorakritos (5th century BC), a votive relief of Triptolemos, a headless statue of Asklepios (4th century BC) and the colossal statue of Kore with *kiste* (a sacred casket) on her head.

Last, also exhibited in the museum are replicas of important finds, such as the painted terracotta pinax of Ninnion, which was dedicated to Demeter and Persephone, the relief with representation of Demeter, Persephone and Triptolemos, and the pediment of a treasury of the same period as the Parthenon.

ELEUSIS ARCHAEOLOGICAL MUSEUM
1 GIOKA ST - ELEUSIS
TEL.: 2105546019
TUESDAY - SUNDAY: 9.00-14.30 HRS
MONDAY: CLOSED

Odysseus Blinding Polyphemos

Demeter and Persephone

Reconstruction of the temple of Poseidon

SOUNION

Sounion is located 67 kilometres southeast of Athens, where the Attica peninsula thrusts into the sea. The summit of the headland is crowned by the white columns of the ancient temple of Poseidon, in true harmony with the landscape. This point offers a splendid vista of the coasts of Attica, the offshore islets, the Cyclades and the mountains of the Peloponnese. The sunset here is a magical experience.

The area was evidently inhabited from early times. Graves and other finds attest the existence of a prehistoric settlement in the third millennium BC. Sounion was also a religious centre in early times, since Homer characterizes it as the sacred cape. Many gods and heroes were worshipped there, but Athena and Poseidon were the dominant deities.

The Athenians soon realized the great strategic importance of the promontory and fortified it, in order to control the sea routes towards the islands and, primarily, towards Euboea, along which sailed the cargo ships laden with grain for the sustenance of the population of Athens. Above all, however, they were anxious to protect the major source of their wealth, the mines of argentiferous lead ores in the neighbouring Laureotike, the income from which enabled them to build, at Themistocles' behest, the 200 trieremes with which they crushed the Persian fleet at Salamis in 480 BC. To this end, the Athenians built on top of the cape a semicircular wall, about 500 metres long and 3 metres thick, reinforced by square towers at 20-metre intervals. On the seaward northwest side they dug into the rock

and built a small shipyard for two triremes, which patrolled the area, protected the cape and guarded it against possible enemy attack.

The sanctuary of Poseidon is entered through the Propylaia on the northeast side. To the right lie the ruins of a square room, which was possibly the guardhouse, and the ruins of two porticoes at right angle to each other, in which devotees sheltered during festivals, particularly in the event of bad weather.The temple of Poseidon was built in the mid-fifth century BC, to replace the old poros temple that had fallen victim to the Persian mayhem in 480 BC. The white marble comes from the quarries at Agrileza, not far from Sounion, on Lauriotic Olympos. This marble is not of the same composition as the Pentelic marble of Athens and does not have the warm golden glow distinctive of the Acropolis monuments. It is, moreover, less resilient and is susceptible to erosion by the briny sea breeze. For this reason the architect made shallower flutes on the column shafts and reduced their number from 20 to 16. Although the architect of the temple is unknown, he must have been the same one as built the temple of Hephaistos and Ares in the ancient Agora of Athens, and the temple of Nemesis at Rhamnous.

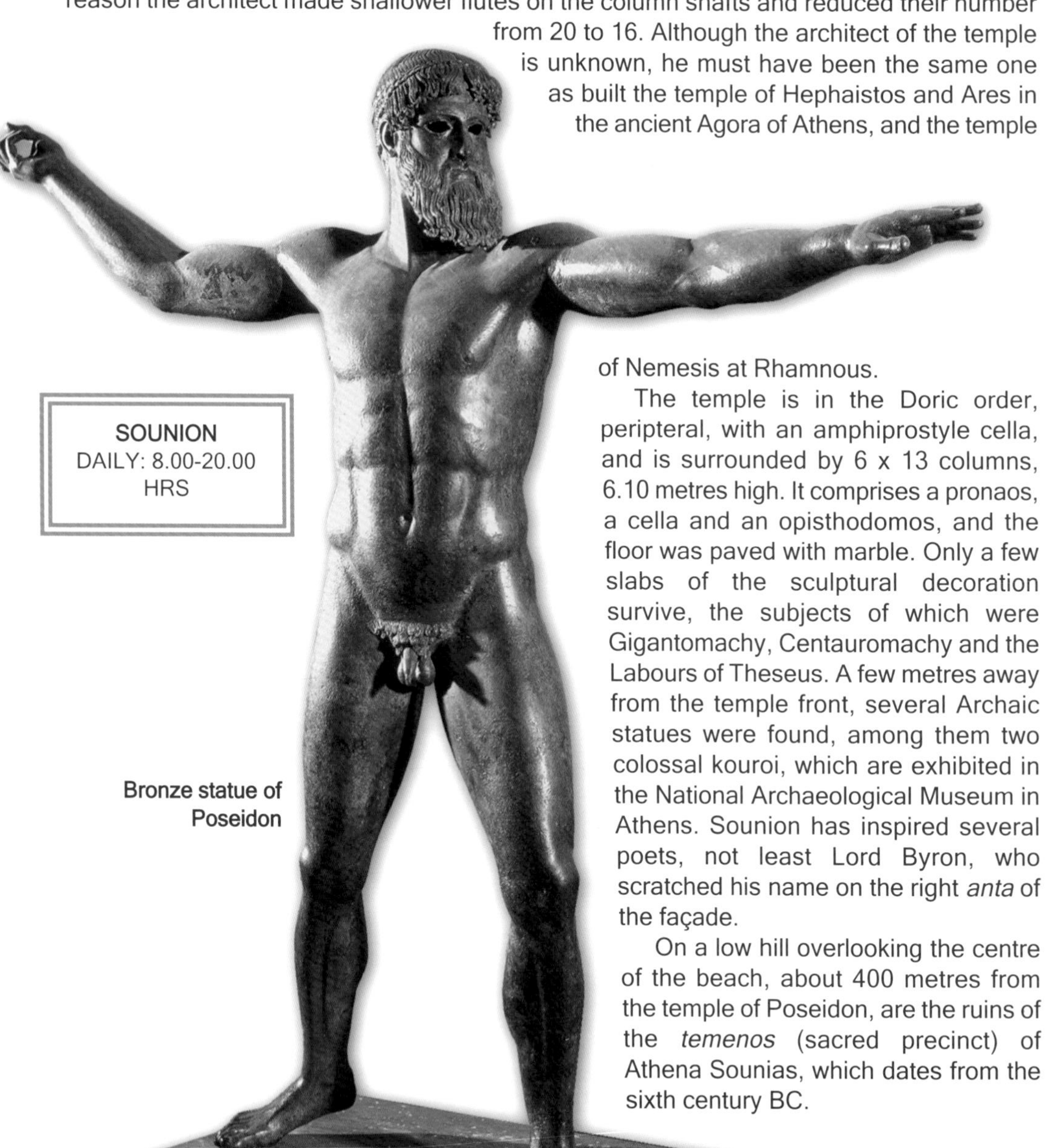

Bronze statue of Poseidon

SOUNION
DAILY: 8.00-20.00 HRS

The temple is in the Doric order, peripteral, with an amphiprostyle cella, and is surrounded by 6 x 13 columns, 6.10 metres high. It comprises a pronaos, a cella and an opisthodomos, and the floor was paved with marble. Only a few slabs of the sculptural decoration survive, the subjects of which were Gigantomachy, Centauromachy and the Labours of Theseus. A few metres away from the temple front, several Archaic statues were found, among them two colossal kouroi, which are exhibited in the National Archaeological Museum in Athens. Sounion has inspired several poets, not least Lord Byron, who scratched his name on the right *anta* of the façade.

On a low hill overlooking the centre of the beach, about 400 metres from the temple of Poseidon, are the ruins of the *temenos* (sacred precinct) of Athena Sounias, which dates from the sixth century BC.

BRAURON

On the east shore of Attica, lapped by the waters of the South Euboean Gulf, is the area of Brauron, famed in Antiquity for the sanctuary of Artemis Brauronia. This goddess was worshipped as protectress of animals and of the countryside, and as helpmeet of women in the hour of childbirth.

The area of Brauron was settled in Neolithic times (3500 BC), flourished in the Middle Helladic, the Early Mycenaean and the Late Helladic period (2000-1000 BC), and then fell into decline. However, archaeological finds attest that by the ninth century BC the area was enjoying a new lease of life. It was in these years that the sanctuary was founded. The large temple dedicated to Artemis was built in the fifth century BC, in the Doric order, on the site of an earlier Archaic one. All that remains today is part of its foundation.

Preserved in better condition is a Π-shaped stoa in the Doric order, with internal court open towards the temple. This stoa was erected *circa* 425-415 BC and is known as the 'Stoa of the Arktoi', because here lived the '*arktoi*' (Gr. bears), that is little girls and boys of 5-10 years old, whose parents had made a vow to the goddess that the children would serve her for a period. The stoa had nine rooms, each of which held eleven beds. From representations in vase-painting it is deduced that the '*arktoi*' took part in the festivals celebrated in Artemis' honour. The most important festival was the Brauronia, which were held every four years. In addition to the rites and contests, it included the procession that commenced from the sanctuary of Artemis on the Acropolis and terminated at the sanctuary of Brauron. To the west of the sanctuary and the stoa are the ruins of an ancient stone bridge that spanned the River Erasinos, and nearby are the ruins of a three-aisled Early Christian basilica of the fifth century AD.

THE BRAURON ARCHAEOLOGICAL MUSEUM

This museum is one of the most important in Attica and houses a wealth of impressive finds from the sanctuary of Artemis Brauronia, such as jewellery, sculptures, sealstones, vases, many inscriptions, terracotta figurines of Artemis, votive reliefs with representations of worship of the goddess, and statues of '*arktoi*'.

The Brauron Archaeological Museum also houses finds from the cemeteries in the surrounding areas, such as Anavyssos, Merenda and Perati (Porto Rafti).

A 'Bear' *(Arktos)*

SANCTUARY OF BRAURON
BRAURON - ATTICA
TEL.: 2299027020
TUESDAY - SUNDAY: 8.30-15.00 HRS
MONDAY: CLOSED

Votive relief from the sanctuary

MARATHON

Some 30 kilometres outside Athens is the town of Marathon. Situated in a landscape with a rich prehistoric and historical past, it too is one of the important archaeological sites in Attica. Many archaeological finds from the area document its habitation from Neolithic times.

At the localities of Tsepi and Vrana there are two prehistoric cemeteries. At the locality Brexiza there are two significant monuments, the sanctuary of the Egyptian Gods, where life-size and colossal statues were found, and the *balneum* (bathhouse) of Herodes Atticus, of the second century AD, in which portrait busts of Roman emperors were uncovered.

The most important monuments at Marathon are the Tumuli of the Athenians and the Plataiaians who fell in the battle of Marathon. These are two manmade mounds of earth and stones covering graves. The tumuli were raised to commemorate the 192 Athenians and Plataiaians who lost their life fighting against the Persians in 490 BC. Not only did the Greeks defeat the Persians in the famous battle that took place in the Marathon Plain, they also dispelled the myth of Persian invincibility. The Tumulus of the Athenians is 9 metres high, approximately 185 metres in circumference and 50 metres in diameter. The Tumulus of the Plataiaians is 4 metres high and 30 metres in diameter.

The Marathon Archaeological Museum stands close to the site of Vrana. Exhibits include vases from the prehistoric settlements and graves in the area. Noteworthy are grave stelai of the Classical and Roman periods, statues from the sanctuary of the Egyptian gods, statues of Herodes Atticus and of members of the imperial family.

TUMULUS OF MARATHON
MARATHON - ATTICA
TEL.: 2294055462
TUESDAY - SUNDAY: 8.30-15.00 HRS
MONDAY: CLOSED

RHAMNOUS

Rhamnous was a *demos* of the Aiantis tribe. It takes its name from the Greek word *rhamnos*, a thorny plant that thrived in the area. It is the best-preserved ancient *demos* in Attica, on the northeast coast, facing the Euboean Gulf. The important archaeological site of Rhamnous includes, among other monuments, the ruins of the sanctuary of the goddess Nemesis.

Archaeological finds attest that the area was inhabited from the Neolithic Age. On entering the archaeological site, visitors see the tomb enclosures and the tomb monuments of Menestides and Euphranor. As they progress, they pass a farmhouse with various spaces, to the north of which stood the temple of Nemesis. The first Archaic temple was built in the early sixth century BC. At the end of the century it was replaced by another temple of poros stone in the Doric order, which was destroyed by the Persians in 479 BC. A small temple was erected in its place in the early fifth century BC.

In the middle years of the fifth century BC, the large peristyle temple of Nemesis was constructed. It had six columns on the narrow sides and twelve on the long sides, but some parts of it remained unfinished. There was no sculptural decoration on the metopes and pediments, in contrast to the apical and corner akroteria, which were adorned with compositions and chimaeras. Inside the temple, at the far end of the cella, stood the Parian marble statue of Nemesis, work of the sculptor Agorakritos, pupil of Pheidias. This statue and its relief base survive in hundreds of fragments. Christian fanatics destroyed the temple and shattered the statue in the late fourth century AD.

Preserved to the east of the temple are the foundations of an altar, to the north of which was a wooden stoa and in front of it a fountain. At a distance of 600 metres from the sanctuary of Nemesis, on the beach of Rhamnous, a large fort with fortification wall 800 metres in length was built in the fifth century BC. This was used for surveillance of shipping in the Gulf of Euboea, particularly of the grain ships bound for Athens. The upper and the lower part of the fort are separated by a wall with gateway. In the upper part are the installations of the garrison, while in the lower part are the theatre, the gymnasium, the sanctuary of Dionysos, public buildings and the sanctuary of the Hero Archegetes.

OROPOS, THE AMPHIAREION

In a densely wooded ravine, in an enchanting landscape about 5 kilometres northwest of the village of Kalamos in Attica, is the archaeological site of the Amphiareion or Amphiaraeion.

Here were discovered the ruins of the sanctuary of the divine hero Amphiaraos, who was also a great seer and took part in the campaign of the Seven Against Thebes. He suffered a tragic end, when his chariot disappeared into a chasm opened in the earth where it was struck by lightning sent by Zeus.

The sanctuary was founded for mainly religious purposes in the late fifth century BC and the festivals of the Great and the Lesser Amphiareia were established at the same time. The Great Amphiareia were held every four years and included athletics and equestrian games, and music contests. The Lesser Amphiareia were an annual festival. Excavations at the site were conducted by the Greek Archaeological Society in the years 1884 to 1929.

On entering the sanctuary, visitors see on the left pedestals of statues of Hellenistic and Roman times, seven of which are signed. On the right are remnants of the temple of Amphiaraos, which was built in the fourth century BC, in the Doric order, with pronaos and cella. Inside the temple stood the marble statue of the god. In front of the temple was a therapeutic spring and a large altar dedicated to gods. North of the altar were semicircular stone steps on which worshippers could sit and watch the sacrifices and other events. Behind the stoa was the theatre of the sanctuary, constructed in the second century BC. It had a wooden *cavea* that could accommodate 4,000 spectators, and a semicircular, two-storey *skene*, of which the proscenium has been restored. The sanctuary precinct also included a bathhouse for women, hostels, shops, auxiliary buildings, houses and a hydraulic clock.

AMPHIAREION
KALAMOS - ATTICA
TEL.: 2295062144
TUESDAY - SUNDAY: 8.30-15.00 HRS
MONDAY: CLOSED

ΚΑΡΠΟΥΖΙ
65

THE SARONIC GULF

Since Antiquity this has been the best-known gulf of Greece, on the shores of which several historical cities and places of worship developed. It takes its name from the mythical king of Troezen, Saron, and is formed by the west coast of Attica, the coast of the Megaris and the east coast of the Corinthia and the Argolid. In the Saronic Gulf lie the islands of Aegina, Salamis, Poros and Hydra, and many islets.

AEGINA

Reconstruction of the temple of Aphaia

The beginnings of the history of Aegina are lost in the mists of time. Certainly, it was inhabited in the Neolithic Age, by settlers from the Peloponnese.

The island's first name was Oinone. Tradition has it that it was named Aegina when Zeus, or according to another version Aias, abducted the daughter of the river-god Asopos, Aegina, and took her to the island, where she gave birth to Aiakos, renowned for his justice. The island's inhabitants were successful merchants and mariners, ploughing the seas of the Eastern Mediterranean, as far as the Euxine Pontus (Black Sea). In the sixth century BC they minted the first silver coins, known as 'turtles', which together with the weights and measures of Aegina were disseminated throughout the Mediterranean and kept their value until Roman times. Aegina was destroyed because of its rivalry with Athens and from 390 BC it is mentioned only circumstantially in history.

Many monuments of various periods exist on the island, but the most important is, without doubt, the temple of Aphaia, which tops a hill about 300 metres high, overlooking the bay of Agia Marina. The cult of Aphaia seems to have been introduced from Crete (where she was known also as Britomartis Cretan Artemis and Diktynna), when trading relations were established between the two islands. According to myth, Aphaia was a noble maiden from Crete, who, in order to escape the amorous advances of Minos, boarded an Aeginetan ship. However, because there too she was harassed by the sailors, she leapt into the sea, was washed ashore on Aegina and vanished into the woods, where she became '*a phaia*', which means ‘invisible’ or ‘unseen’.

The temple of Aphaia was built in the early fifth century BC. Peripteral and in the Doric order, it is 15.50 metres wide and 30.50 metres long, with six columns on the narrow sides and twelve on the long ones. It has a pronaos and an opisthodomos *in antis*, which communicated with the cella in which stood the cult statue of the goddess, protected by wooden railings. The temple is built of local poros stone, except for the pediments and the roof, which were of marble. Of the poros columns, 5.27 metres high, some are monolithic and others consist of drums.

The sculptural decoration of the two pediments represented scenes from the two Trojan campaigns, in which the members of the house of Aiakas distinguished themselves. At the centre of both is the figure of Athena, and arranged symmetrically on either side of the goddess are Herakles’ battles against Trojans, on the east pediment, and Agamemnon fighting against Trojans, on the west. Only seventeen of these statues have been unearthed and can be seen today in the Munich Glyptothek.

Detail of a column of the temple

POROS

This island in the Saronic Gulf was known in Antiquity as Kalauria. It is only a short distance from Piraeus and is separated from Troezinia by a narrow sea channel, which facilitates regular communication by ferryboat. Poros is a picturesque island, with lovely sandy beaches, verdant vegetation and several places of interest. Its capital, also called Poros, is a quaint town with narrow streets, traditional shops and hospitable people. Among the places that merit a visit are the Archaeological Museum, with the statues of the Classical period from ancient Troezenia and the island, the main square with the clock-tower, from which there is an excellent view of the harbour and the area of Galatas opposite, and the Lemonodasos (= Lemon Wood), the most fragrant corner in Greece. Poros is a popular tourist haunt.

HYDRA

The island to the west of the entrance to the Saronic Gulf is said to have been inhabited first by Dryopians or Dolopians. On the site of the present capital, ruins of the ancient city of 'Hydrea' have been found. Hydra is very attractive with distinctive traditional architecture. Its grand mansions with their tiled roofs and their courtyards, their interior furnishings and decoration, give visitors the impression of stepping back in time. Noteworthy among the island's sights are the stone-built mansions around the harbour, which date from the eighteenth century and

today house an Old People's Home, the hostel of the Advanced School of Fine Arts of the National Technical University of Athens, and the Officer Cadets' Academy of the Merchant Navy. The cannon emplacements beside the harbour are a reminder of the island's role in the 1821 War of Independence. There is also a museum with an archive of the feats of Hydraian sailors against the Ottoman Turks. Hydra is one of the most highly developed tourist islands in Greece, with a sophisticated, cosmopolitan ambience. No automobiles are allowed and the beautiful beaches can be reached only by caique.

The house of poet Angelos Sikelianos

The stone lighthouse of the island

The theatre of Euripides

SALAMIS

Salamis, the largest island in the Saronic Gulf, lies at its north end and is separated from Attica by the straits of Perama (east) and Pachi (northwest). Much of the island is covered by pine woods.

Myth has it that the island was named after Salamis, daughter of the river-god Asopos, wife of Poseidon and mother of Kychreus. One of Kychreus' daughters married Aias (Ajax), who became king of Salamis. The island was a bone of contention between the Athenians and the Megarians. From the late seventh century BC it belonged to the Megarians, until *circa* 570 BC. It then passed to the domination of the Athenians, until 318 BC, when it was captured by the Macedonians. However, in 229 BC it returned to the Athenians.

Many Mycenaean tombs have been found at various points on the island. The ruins of the agora, of the temple of Aias, the altar of the twelve gods, the exhedra, the gymnasium, temples, sanctuaries and the portrait statue of Solon are some of the archaeological finds brought to light on Salamis.

The island is renowned also for the naval battle fought in 480 BC, when the Greek fleet under the command of Themistocles confronted the Persian fleet under Xerxes, in the narrows of Salamis, close to the coast. The Greeks had a resounding victory.

Despite the building boom on Salamis in recent years, the island has kept much of its charm and the remarkable natural beauty of its shores.

SPETSES

Spetses is the westernmost island in the Argosaronic Gulf and lies very close to the south coast of the Argolid. In ancient times it was known as Pityousa, which means forested with pines. Archaeological finds indicate that the island was settled in Early Helladic and Mycenaean times. The capital town is well-kept and attractive, with many scheduled buildings. The streets are narrow and the houses are characteristic of the island architecture.

There are many sights of interest on Spetses. In Dapia Square are the cannon used by the Spetsiots to defend their island. The residence of the nobleman Hadjigiannis-Mexis now houses a museum in which the bones of Bouboulina, heroine of the Greek War of Independence, are kept and folk art exhibits, heirlooms of 1821, as well as letters of Theodoros Kolokotronis and Athanasios Diakos, are on display. Visitors can enjoy looking at the several little churches and the mansions on the coasts of the island. The lovely clean beaches are mainly in the south part. With its tranquil natural beauty and its very good tourism infrastructure, Spetses is a favourite haunt of Greek and foreign holidaymakers. To the south of Spetses is a small, privately-owned island with lush vegetation, Spetsopoula.

Bouboulina

ELEFSIN
SALAMINA
SARONIC GULF
EGINA
POROS
YDRA
SPETSES

OROPOS
RAMNOUNTAS
MARATHONAS
AFNI
ATHINA
KESARIANI
REAS
VRAVRONA
SOUNIO

ATHENS PUBLIC TRANSPORTATION MAP

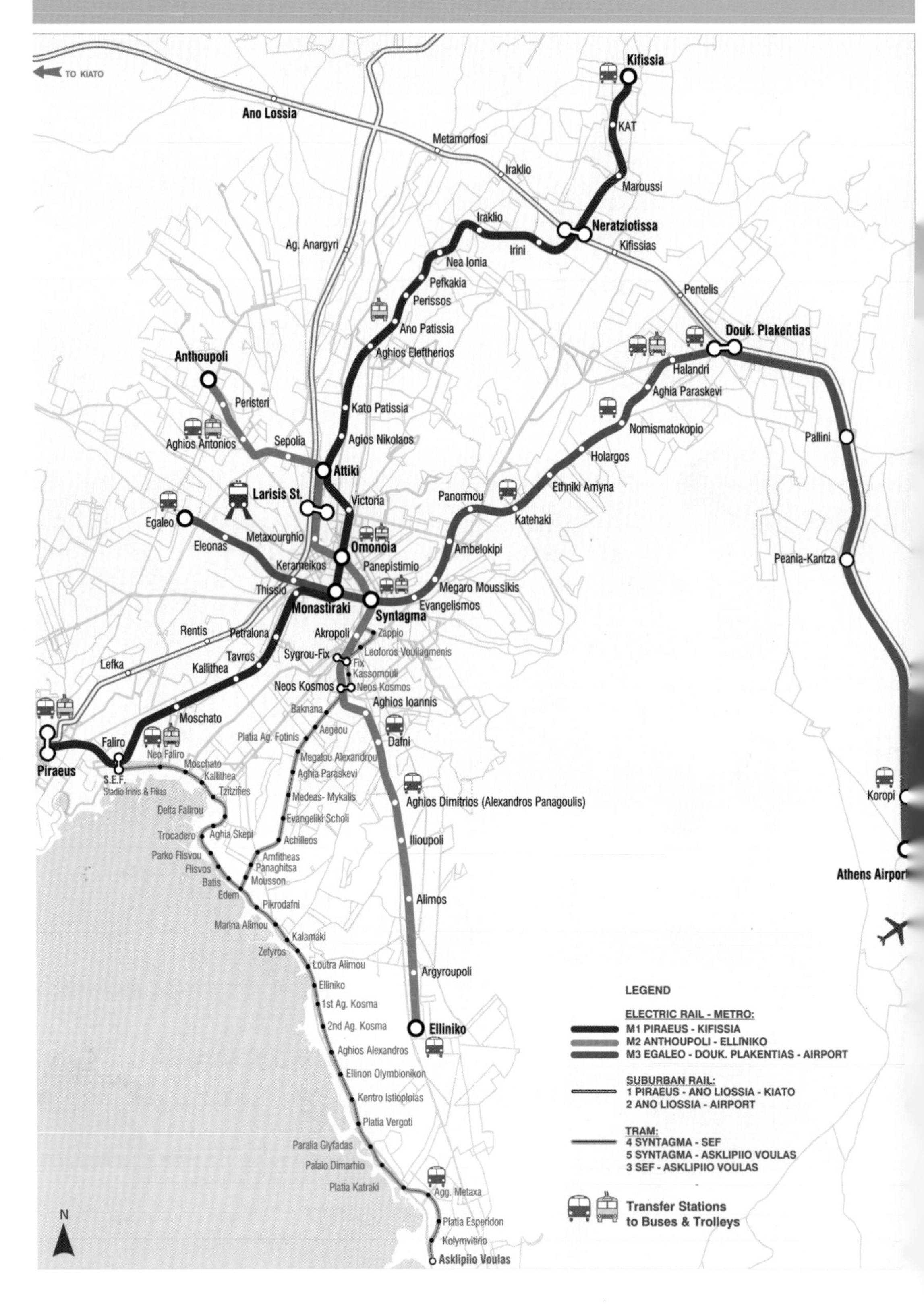